The Southern Coastal Heritage Program
North Carolina State University Humanities Extension/Publications

Life at the Edge of the Sea

Essays on North Carolina's Coast and Coastal Culture

(Volume I)

edited by Candy Beal and Carmine Prioli

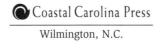

Coastal Carolina Press
Wilmington, N.C.

Life at the Edge of the Sea: Essays on North Carolina's Coast and Coastal Culture
Edited by Candy Beal and Carmine Prioli

⬤ Coastal Carolina Press
www.coastalcarolinapress.org

First Edition 2002.

Book design and production by Whitline Ink Incorporated.
Southern Coastal Heritage Workshop logo design by Susan White.
Cover photograph by Alan Watson.

Printed in the United States of America. ✹
Printed on recycled paper using soy-based inks.

10   9   8   7   6   5   4   3   2   1

Applied for Library of Congress Cataloging-in-Publication Data.

ISBN 1-928556-37-X

Acknowledgments

We wish to thank the staff of the Trinity Center, especially Jacque Mason, for providing the natural and social environments that consistently have contributed to the success of our workshops. Thanks, too, go to the staff of Coastal Carolina Press, particularly to its director, Dr. Andrew Scott, for his early encouragement of this collection of essays, and to Emily Colin for her editorial direction. For their financial support, we are grateful to Dr. Charlie Ewen, director of the Southern Coastal Heritage Program, and to Dr. Jim Clark, director of NCSU's Humanities Extension/Publications. Finally, we want to express our appreciation to all of the contributors to *Life at the Edge of the Sea*. That heterogeneous group includes the authors whose essays appear in this volume and our participants, whose workshop comments and enthusiasm have, over the years, helped develop those essays.

—*Candy Beal and Carmine Prioli*

*F*or their enduring support of The Southern Coastal Heritage Program, this volume is dedicated to **Sondra L. Kirsch** and **W. Keats Sparrow**.

"Always the edge of the sea remains an elusive and indefinable boundary."

—*Rachel Carson*

Contents

Introduction
Our Coast of Many Colors

A decade ago, a small group of preservation-minded citizens assembled at North Carolina State University to discuss their concerns for coastal North Carolina. New, ambitious road construction projects would soon slice through Piedmont and coastal plain farmlands, laying down ribbons of asphalt that would swell the numbers of vacationers flooding to the coast. The group, which included educators, administrators, archivists, and private citizens, debated the effects that this march to the sea would have on the fabric of coastal life. Already, vast stretches of barrier islands had been covered with condos. Sleepy villages had been strip-developed with fast food joints and convenience stores. Given this form of "progress," the group collectively wondered what would become of the decoy carvers and the sea chantey singers, the boat builders, the commercial fishermen and their families. How could citizens everywhere be best taught about our coastal treasures and heritage? What could be done to foster a sense of appreciation and stewardship among visitors to the coast? How could natives of the coast themselves pass on their cultural traditions to succeeding generations of beachgoers and residents alike?

The N.C. State group had no firm answers to these difficult questions, but they agreed on one thing: the best and quickest way to educate North Carolina's schoolchildren about coastal issues was to educate their teachers. They decided that a residential workshop—perhaps a series of them—might at least begin the work of fostering an appreciation for the challenges facing our traditional coastal communities. And thus was conceived a program called the Southern Coastal Heritage Workshop for Educators.

The first workshop was held in the summer of 1993 at the Trinity Conference Center, located on Emerald Isle in Salter Path, North Carolina. Since then, we have offered eight additional workshops—all at the Trinity Center—and another is planned as this book is going to press. Judging from teachers' follow-up comments, they have found the workshops to be a resounding success, and have enjoyed the program's hands-on, shoes-off approach to learning. "Lectures" are often on site, at a carver's knee or knee-deep in estuarine muck. Our consultants come from just about every place and perspective: university professors, scientists, storytellers, ballad singers, decoy carvers, fishermen. They talk both from the head and the heart, sharing history, theories,

Workshop participants learn how to use a sweep net in Bogue Sound. (All photos in this section courtesy of Southern Coastal Heritage Program.)

and passionate beliefs built on years of coastal experience. It's that experience and homegrown knowledge that we prompt our participants to capture. More important, it's that experience that we hope they transmit to their many colleagues back home (to whom the teachers are expected to report) and, in turn, to the thousands of students who are subsequently taught lessons based on workshop information.

Partly as a result of the success of the teacher workshops, North Carolina State University, East Carolina University, the University of North Carolina at Wilmington, the University of North Carolina Sea Grant Program, and the North Carolina Division of Cultural Resources have formally established the Southern Coastal Heritage Program. Through this program, the sponsoring institutions seek to promote coastal heritage around the state. The workshop is presently one of the projects this group oversees. Other projects include presentations and support for coastal research, and coastal publications, including this volume of essays, directed toward educators and the general public.

Life at the Edge of the Sea responds to the many requests we have had from our workshop alumni and others to "write it down." That is, assemble in compact, book form the information, experiences, lessons, and personalities that have made the workshops "work" for all of us—planners, contributors, and participants. After several futile efforts to imagine how something as diverse and multi-faceted as our workshops would appear in a single volume, we elected to keep it relatively simple. We asked a few of our "old hands,"

Susan Lovelace, education coordinator at the N.C. National Estuarine Resource Reserve, discusses the anatomy of the fiddler crab.

mostly professors who are adept at this sort of thing, to "write it down," to record and perhaps expand upon some of their individual contributions to the workshop. Lacking a ready resource for one area we believed essential—early history of Native Americans on the coast—we invited a newcomer to our group, Professor Randy Daniel, to address that important subject.

Stan Riggs always opens the workshop. He is known throughout the state for his depth of knowledge about the geology of the coast and its evolution over time. His approach to understanding North Carolina's coastal system includes an ocean-to-estuary march across Emerald Isle that combines direct observation with common sense and hard science. Just as he does at the workshop, in his essay, "Life at the Edge of North Carolina's Coastal System: The Geologic Controls," Riggs positions our study of the coast, its origin and its complexities, in its largest context. He dispels the myth that the barrier islands are fragile. Instead, he describes them as energy absorbers, built to roll over again and again. They will last as long as there are sand, wind, water, and tidal currents. It's the fixed human structures that are fragile, and Riggs's essay offers solid reasons to support the belief that we are "loving our coastal system to death."

Lundie Spence was the first workshop consultant who took us into waist-deep water to discover the workings of an estuary. With her, we have seined the waters of Bogue Sound, magnified its droplets, and mucked about with blue crabs, shrimp, and the lowly sea squirt amid floating detritus and coarse cordgrasses. In her essay, "Estuaries: Where the River Meets the Ocean," you may feel this same sense of discovery as you explore what she calls "these vast natural treasures," nearly 4,000 miles of estuarine shoreline in North Carolina alone.

In "Archaeology and Ancient Cultures at the Edge of the Sea," Randy Daniel takes us into the realm of early Native American history. Most of us are familiar with John White's watercolors and Thomas Harriot's descriptions of sixteenth-century Native Americans, but we don't have a great deal of knowledge about Native American culture dating from this era. Through fieldwork and "thoughtful interpretation," finding meaning in rocks, bones, and pottery fragments, Daniel is in the process of recovering their story. His research has led to new discoveries in the search for our earliest "lost colonies," for which no written records exist.

Most visitors to the beach are unaware that some of the roads they travel on were once Native American trade routes. These roads, which reach so far back into the past, can also carry us into the future. Longtime visitors to North Carolina's coast will recognize changes in the color and sound of the human landscape. Based on years of research he has done in maritime communities along the eastern seaboard, David Griffith's "Coasts in the Works: Impressions of Working Waterfronts" places these changes within both larger and more personal contexts.

Griffith was the first of our consultants to discuss the changing culture that migrant laborers bring to our coast. His essay examines the efforts these laborers make to assimilate into coastal culture, while at the same time remaining true to their origins. Griffith asks hard questions about our willingness to embrace the social diversity of the migrant culture as a source of economic and creative growth.

"Speech at the Beach: The Outer Banks Brogue" by Walt Wolfram is a revealing look at the unique speech found on the coast, especially on Ocracoke Island. Wolfram helps us understand the complexities of speech patterns and why pinpointing dialect origins is not a simple matter. He briefly describes the BBC's efforts to trace the brogue back to the days of Shakespeare, and explains that if the brogue is your interest, off-season is the best time to hear it. In the summer, when tourists outnumber islanders ten to one, visitors are more likely to hear North Carolina Piedmont or southern Virginia speech than the Outer Banks brogue. Wolfram and his students have collected speech samples from many places and for many seasons. He is highly regarded by the local people with whom he works. Through the curricular materials he produces and offers to them, he, in turn, provides them with a renewed appreciation for their own heritage and sense of place.

Jim Clark, well known throughout the state for his work as North Carolina State University's Director of Humanities Extension, visited local schools and polled youngsters about their heroes. When asked whom they most admired, few cited the local leaders or community "heroes" who make life better for their communities. Instead, basketball players and rock singers topped their lists. In "'Writing's the main thing': Imaginative Coastal Literature for Young Readers," Clark introduces us to a host of literary characters who, in their individual ways, exhibit some form of heroic behavior and who pose the question: "What, in times of crisis, can a young person do?" They respond with action and, to a young reader wondering, "Who am I and what's my place in the world?" these characters portray heroes in the making.

In "Boat Building the Harkers Island Way," Carmine Prioli cites a local folk belief: "Take a 'youngern' off the island at birth and raise him far inland…When he's about sixteen, just turn him loose in a workshop with pine and juniper. Without plans or instructions of any sort, he'll automatically assemble something with a flared bow, a wide beam, and a 4:1 sheer…" In other words, a traditional Harkers Island workboat, the design of which is "embedded in [his] genes." In addition to citing a bit of coastal folklore, Prioli traces traditional boat construction through its heyday during the 1950s–1970s, when there was a new boat underway in nearly every yard. At the summer workshop, Prioli uses boats and boat building to introduce participants to a culture more attuned to seasonal changes, salt-water currents, and lunar phases than to experience derived from "virtual" reality.

In "African Americans by the Sea," Walt Wolfram looks at the important role African Americans played in the development of the coastal waterways. He tells the story of the Pea Island Lifesaving Station's heroic crew, and of those who served the community by operating small passenger and freight boats between Morehead City and Beaufort. Wolfram points out the difficulties inherent in finding racial balance in the days of Jim Crow and maintaining families in communities that offered limited opportunities for African Americans. He addresses the dilemmas faced by children forced to choose between staying with their families or moving off the Banks to find employment and break old racial stereotypes and rules.

Finally, in "The Stormy Birth of Cape Lookout National Seashore," Carmine Prioli traces the sequence of events that led to the preservation of fifty-five miles of North Carolina's coastline. He describes the strained relationships between the local people and the federal government. Prioli also points to recent initiatives that have replaced mistrust with cooperation and coexistence. The birth of the Cape Lookout National Seashore is a fascinating story. Those of us who cherish the unspoiled vistas that surround Cape Lookout and Shackleford Banks will understand how close we all came to losing access to these natural areas.

Although *Life at the Edge of the Sea* contains only essays from the academic contributors to the workshop, we hope it will honor *all* of our consultants, who are treasures themselves. Individuals like Rodney Kemp have entertained us and "told the news" of Down East culture. Folklife specialist and musician Connie Mason has offered traditional ballads and original compositions on themes ranging from the challenges of eating a raw oyster to the gruesome end of Blackbeard. Park rangers Karen Duggan and Lori Heupel have introduced us to the history and ecology of Cape Lookout, still one of the most pristine stretches of seascape in the United States. We always close the workshop with B.J. White's unforgettable series of demonstrations on Native American hide tanning, tool making, and cooking. There have been other wonderful facilitators, of course, like decoy carvers David Lawrence, Jonathan Willis, Jason Michels, and Caroline Corwin; fisherman and shrimper Zack Davis; naturalists and con-servationists; river keepers and bay watchers. They come from different backgrounds and age groups, but they all have this in common: they are gifted teachers with a pas-sion for the coast's culture, environment, and inhabitants.

These consultants have much to share with all of us and have worked tirelessly to support the preservation of coastal culture. While we recognize that the preservation effort most directly affects coastal residents, coastal culture is, in fact, a heritage shared by everyone. Ultimately, in the workshop we all ask ourselves the same questions: Who are we and what is our place in the world? What shapes us and makes us uniquely North Carolinians? Do we demonstrate self-reliance and an ability to live in har-mony with nature, qualities common to long-time coastal

(ABOVE) *National Park Service Ranger and historian Karen Duggan speaks to participants at the Cape Lookout lighthouse.*

(BELOW) *Singer and N.C. Maritime Museum folklife specialist Connie Mason blends history and coastal dialect into musical entertainment.*

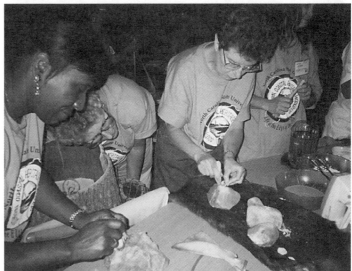

(ABOVE) *B.J. White, Trinity Center educator and curriculum developer, about to conduct a class on Native American cooking.*

(ABOVE RIGHT) *B.J. demonstrates a Native American basket made from a single sheet of tree bark.*

(RIGHT) *Workshop participants try their hands at making wampum as others mix batter for cattail pancakes.*

residents? Are we keepers of our history, stewards for tomorrow's North Carolinians?

It has been my pleasure to serve as the director of the Southern Coastal Heritage Workshop for nine years. I have had the opportunity to work closely with nearly all of the authors whose essays make up this volume. When Jim Clark's plans have allowed, he has served as co-director, and no matter how heavily scheduled he has been, he always found time to share information about coastal literature with the workshop participants.

Carmine Prioli has come each summer to lend a hand, talk about boats, and spin stories that capture the flavor of the coast and its people. Over the years, we have added other topics and have even bowed to the computer age. Now during each workshop, we prepare a virtual scrapbook of the coast. We understand that not all schoolchildren can put their toes in the Atlantic, but thanks to the workshop, their teachers can. With pictures, stories, and this virtual field trip, the teachers can spark the imaginations of their students. To date we have hosted 240 participants who have returned to faculties that number 12,000 and who, in turn, have touched 600,000

(ABOVE) *Workshop participants about to walk the beach on Core Banks in search of sea turtle nests, shells, and other forms of coastal wildlife.*

Three of our younger consultants demonstrate their skills:

(BELOW LEFT) *Zack Davis, commercial fisherman, knits a net he will use while trawling for shrimp.*

(ABOVE LEFT, BELOW RIGHT) *Jason Michels and Caroline Corwin display examples of their prize-winning decoys.*

Zack began nighttime trawling at the age of twelve. Caroline and Jason took up decoy carving in their early teens. The work of these young people indicates that traditional coastal culture, though perilously threatened, is not yet a thing of the past.

students. Have we reached them all? We would like to think so. While we can't guarantee that we have, we're excited about the ongoing possibilities for raising awareness of coastal issues among our children and throughout our state.

I would like to share with you a statement Jim Clark composed for us as we began our journey. A decade ago, Jim wrote:

> *If there ever was a melting pot in the coastal South of the United States, what can we still find in that cracked old cauldron these days? From Maryland to Texas this question is stirring up appetites. One reason for the general curiosity is that economic change and employment options have been cooking down the distinctive old coastal cultures of this complex region into one culture. At least it appears that the historic marine and agrarian ways of life have nearly all been reduced to manufacturing and technology jobs. Wages have gone up, we hear; but old and young people have been left out of the financial tides of the region. Folks have fled inland to work as others have flocked out there to play. In this process, hundreds of local communities, it is said, have gone to the same modern hell.*
>
> *But in the coastal region of the American South, the old ways are not yet gone. Still audible above the cricket sounds of all those computer chips that run the smart new boats is the hum of a prior and persisting existence, and this hum calls us to study and preserve what we can.*
>
> *We see upon examination that up to now Harkers Island is not Edenton any more than Kansas City is Topeka. Far more than local speech patterns still distinguish Beaufort, North Carolina, from Beaufort, South Carolina. We do have time left to record and in some cases to preserve cultural diversity and pluralism. It is time, however, to ask ourselves: Can we clearly make our case for this coastal region as a coast of many colors and cultures before it does all run together?*
>
> *We believe we can. It is our mission to preserve the record of the southern coastal region of North Carolina before the palatable but perishable heritage is gone. Won't you join us?*

These words reflect the sentiments that guide us today. We remain committed to our mission to preserve and protect North Carolina's coastal heritage. We feel we can do no less for the children and citizens of our state. It is a heritage as varied and brilliant as the people and places who come together to paint a vibrant picture of our coast of many colors.

—*Candy Beal*

Speech at the Beach
The Outer Banks Brogue

— Walt Wolfram —

One of the first things visitors to the coastal islands of North Carolina notice is the natives' speech. In fact, one of the traditional labels for people from the Outer Banks is the term *hoi toiders*, an iconic imitation of one of the distinct vowel pronunciations found in words like *high* and *tide*. Comments about the dialect run the full gamut of opinion. At one extreme, visitors may view the dialect as little more than a quaint artifact of island life on display solely for the bemusement of outsiders. One local storeowner from a longstanding island family recalled the following incident:

> I had a lady in [the store] last week I had a battle with. You might as well say a battle with, because she came up to the counter, and she said, "Speak!"
> I said, "Excuse me?"
> She said, "Speak!"
> I was like, "Do I get a biscuit?"
> She said, "I wanna hear you talk."

(Wolfram and Schilling-Estes 122–123)

By the same token, I have encountered visitors who romanticize the dialect as a retention of Elizabethan English preserved by centuries of isolation. Just a few years ago, a television crew from the BBC showed up on the Outer Banks armed with the plays of William Shakespeare for the residents to read. Their intention was to record the sounds of the bard as they might have fallen from his own lips. Over my objections that this was a romantic stereotype, they persisted and convinced a couple of patient, indulgent islanders to read various passages from Shakespeare.[1] A few weeks later I started getting e-mails from friends around the world about a story on BBC and CNN International claiming that Shakespearean English had been found on the Outer Banks of North Carolina. I was personally horrified that I had failed to convince the film producers of a most basic truth about language—that all living languages were constantly changing—but I also learned a valuable lesson about the strength of preconceived language notions. Outer Banks residents who use the dialect hardly need to be reminded of the stereotypes people have about language; they have typically experienced these stereotypes far too often.

Notwithstanding the unjustified stereotypes about Outer Banks speech, there are still legitimate questions that people have about it. What exactly is this distinct variety of English like—the so-called *brogue*? The term brogue itself is a label borrowed from the Irish word *barroq* meaning "to grab hold, especially with the tongue." This label, as well as others such as *hoi toider*, *Banker speech*, and so forth, are indications of the way this dialect has been set apart from other varieties of English, including those spoken in mainland North Carolina. Where does this speech fit in the dialect puzzle of the United States and beyond North America, and how does it compare with the kinds of English spoken around the world, particularly those in the British Isles? How did it develop to begin with? And what will become of it as the inroads of in-migration and tourism take their toll on the once-isolated communities of the region? This essay will address these questions in light of the past, present, and future of the Outer Banks' unique dialect heritage.

What is the Brogue?

What makes the dialects of coastal North Carolina so unique? To the casual observer, the answer may seem obvious: people from this region simply talk differently; they do not sound anything like their mainland neighbors. When I play samples of speakers from different regions of North Carolina, residents of the Outer Banks are the easiest for listeners to identify. Sorting out the details that make the brogue distinct, however, is a bit more complex than it might appear to the casual observer who is transfixed by a couple of marked pronunciation features.

Dialects are organized on several levels: pronunciation, vocabulary, and grammar. The dialects of the Outer Banks distinguish themselves on all of these levels, even though traits on some levels of organization are more conspicuous than others—especially to visitors but also to the residents themselves, as they have become aware that their dialect is different from others.

The most distinguishing characteristics of pronunciation are several vowel sounds, although there are also more subtle differences that dialectologists cite in their detailed accounts of Outer Banks dialects (e.g., Howren 1962; Jaffe 1973; Wolfram, Hazen, and Schilling-Estes 1999). The most noticeable pronunciation is, of course, the long *i* vowel sound in words like *tide*, *time*, and *high*. Although the Outer Banks pronunciation is often characterized as sounding like the *oy* vowel of *boy* or *toy*, the actual production is more like the combination of the *uh* sound of *but* and the *ee* sound of *beet*, so that the Outer Banks pronunciation of *tide* really sounds something like *t-uh-ee-d*. The Outer Banks is not the only region where this sound occurs. It is characteristic of particular regions in the British Isles and in the English of Australia and New Zealand, and even in some parts of the United States, though it does not nearly receive as much attention in other settings as it does in coastal North Carolina. For example, some New Yorkers use it, though it is rarely commented upon. In the South, including North Carolina, the pronunciation contrasts sharply with the mainland pronunciation in words like *tahm* for *time* or *tahd* for *tide*.

While visitors and Outer Banks residents may focus on the distinctiveness of the *i* sound in *tide*, linguists find other vowels that are just as distinctive. For instance, the Outer Banks production of the vowel in words like *sound* and *brown* is every bit as distinct—perhaps even more so in terms of American English dialects—but it is not usually the focus of attention. The vowel sound in the word *brown* actually sounds closer to the vowel in *brain*, and the vowel sound in *mound* sounds closer to that in *mind*. Outsiders have been known to confuse words like *brown* and *brain* or *mound* and *mind*. In fact, when I isolate and play the traditional Outer Banks pronunciation of the single word *brown* for listeners from different areas and ask them what word it is, they typically say "brain."

Another pronunciation trait, the vowel sound in words like *caught* and *bought,* is produced closer (though not identically) to the vowel sound in words like *put* or *book*, a pronunciation that is unique among the dialects of American English. The pronunciation of this vowel is much more like its production in many British dialects of English than it is like its production in other   North American dialects of English. In fact, it seems to be one of the features that makes outsiders say that the Outer Banks brogue sounds more like British English or Australian English than it does American English, even though most people don't talk about this vowel nearly as much as they do about the vowel of *high tide.*

As it turns out, Americans are not the only ones who think that Outer Banks English sounds more like British dialects than American dialects. A few years ago, Peter Trudgill, an eminent British dialectologist, visited the Outer Banks with staff of the North Carolina Language and Life Project to hear the dialect for himself. He took back with him a sample of Outer Banks speech and played it to a group of fifteen native speakers of British English in Essex, England, located in East Anglia. The listeners were unanimous in attributing the Outer Banks speech sample to a British Isles origin, with most people "opting for an origin in the 'West Country'— that is, southwestern England" (e-mail from Peter Trudgill, 1995).

Most people focus on the pronunciation features of the Outer Banks brogue, but there are also other noteworthy dialect traits found in its vocabulary and grammar. A word of caution is, however, necessary in presenting vocabulary differences. There are actually few words unique to the Outer Banks; in fact, we have found only a couple dozen out of the thousands of dialect words we collected. Words like *meehonkey* or *whoop and holler* for "hide and seek" on Ocracoke, or the special meaning of words for outsiders, like *dit-dot* and *dingbatter* on Harkers Island, as well as terms for local places such as *the ditch* ("mouth of the harbor") or *up the beach* ("off the island") seem to be among the few newly-coined items in these varieties not found elsewhere. There are also some unique nuances of meanings assigned to Outer Banks dialect words that are found in other areas as well. For example, the use of the word *mommuck,* an older English word found in the works of William Shakespeare and retained in some more isolated dialect areas of the United States such as Appalachia in addition to the Outer Banks, has developed a meaning on the Outer Banks that sets it apart from both its original meaning and the meaning it has developed in other regions. In the works of Shakespeare, it is used to refer to "tearing apart" in a literal sense (e.g., *They mommucked the curtain*), whereas on the Outer Banks its meaning has been extended to refer to mental or physical harassment (e.g., *The young'uns were mommucking me*). This meaning is, in turn, distinguished from its meaning in some mainland dialects of southeastern North Carolina. For example, in Robeson County and the western mountain area of the state it means "mess up" (e.g., *They mommucked up the house*).

Dialect words also reinforce an important point about Outer Banks speech: it is the combination

Walt Wolfram conducting a seminar on coastal dialects.
(photo by Herman Lankford, courtesy of North Carolina Language and Life Project)

of the old with the new that defines its current state. Words like *mommuck, quamish,* meaning "upset" as in *quamished in the gut,* and *token of death,* meaning "an unusual sign of impending death" (such as a rooster crowing in the middle of the day) are all words that have been in the English language for centuries. On the other hand, words like *dingbatter* and *dit dot,* terms for "outsiders," are relatively new. In fact, our research on the term *dingbatter* shows that it was adopted from the popular 1970s television sitcom *All in the Family.* In this show, Archie Bunker regularly refers to his wife Edith as a "dingbat" when she displays—in his eyes—a lack of common sense. This item was documented on the Outer Banks in the 1970s when the show was first aired there. Prior to that time, terms like *foreigner* and *stranger* were used to describe outsiders.

Along with a few special but highly symbolic word uses that clearly distinguish outsiders from "insiders," it is important to understand that the vast majority of dialect words found on the Outer Banks are common in other dialect areas, mostly in the South.[2] Of course, there are also dialect words that tend to be associated with marine life and are thus shared by other coastal communities in the Mid-Atlantic area, such as *slick cam* for "smooth water," *winard* for "into the wind," or *lightering* for the activity in which the heavy cargo from large sailing ships was placed on smaller vessels able to navigate in the shallow waters of the Pamlico and Albemarle Sounds.

There are also noteworthy grammatical differences that typify Outer Banks speech, but only a couple that are truly distinctive to this region. The use of *weren't* where other dialects use *wasn't,* as in *I weren't there* or *It weren't in the house* is only found in the Mid-Atlantic coastal region, although its use does extend from the coastal areas of Virginia and Maryland down to the southern areas of coastal North Carolina. The use of the preposition *to* for *at,* as in *She's to the house tonight,* is also fairly limited, though it is found in some other coastal areas of the mid-Atlantic coastal region. The use of an –*s* on verbs in sentences with plural subjects, such as *The dogs barks every night,* is characteristic of the Outer Banks brogue, but it is also found in other historically isolated dialects as well, such as those in Appalachia. The same is true for the use of the *uh* sound before verbs, as in *The duck was a-flying in the sound.* The grammar of the Outer Banks may not add many unique dialect features to the make-up of the dialect, but it is certainly a part of the overall profile that makes Outer Banks English what it is. While pronunciation remains the primary topic of conversation for non-islanders and islanders alike, vocabulary and grammar are essential ingredients for the dialect mix that makes the Outer Banks distinctive.

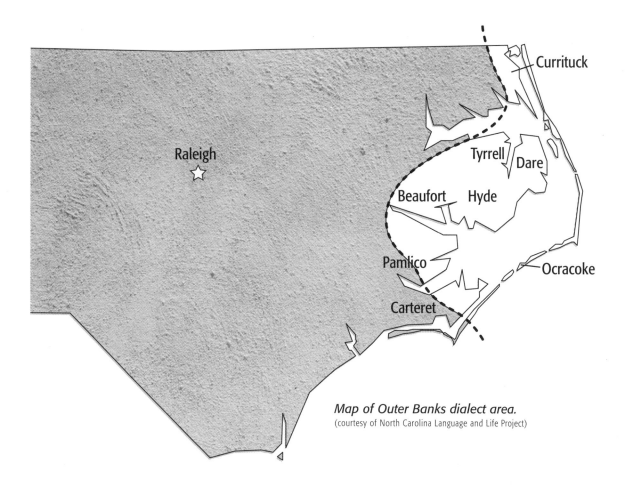

Map of Outer Banks dialect area.
(courtesy of North Carolina Language and Life Project)

Who Speaks the Brogue?

Although the brogue tends to be associated mostly with longstanding, marine-based coastal communities like Ocracoke, Harkers Island, and Wanchese, the boundaries of the dialect area are actually more expansive than that, including parts of the mainland adjacent to the Outer Banks. A map showing the approximate boundaries of the brogue is given above. The line delineating the boundaries, called a *dialect isogloss*, was drawn on the basis of a composite of various dialect surveys that have been conducted over the last half-century, which typically include interviews with a couple of representative speakers in different counties as a part of large-scale surveys. In addition, we used our own surveys of speakers conducted in the 1990s and long-term studies of particular communities such as Ocracoke, Harkers Island, and mainland Hyde County.

The dialect isogloss (or boundary) delimiting the brogue starts at the southern end of the Outer Banks, including Bogue and Core Sounds, and extends northward beyond the North Carolina border into coastal Virginia and Maryland. In fact, people who have visited island communities in the Chesapeake Bay, such as Tangier Island in Virginia and Smith Island in Maryland, readily notice some of the strong similarities, such as the characteristic vowels of *tide* and *sound* and the use of *weren't* where other dialects use *wasn't*. Trained dialectologists and many locals will, of course, notice some peculiarities in the different locations that distinguish them in more subtle ways. As is seen on the map, the dialect also encompasses regions of the mainland bordering the Outer Banks, including all of Hyde County and Dare County and parts of Carteret, Pamlico, and Currituck Counties as well.

While an isogloss marks the boundary of a dialect area, it only gives a partial—and often oversimplified—picture of the dialect region. Even the geographical delimitation is only approximate, because the edges of the dialect boundaries are often quite fuzzy as the brogue fades into the regional dialects of the coastal plains to the west of it. Perhaps more important in the description of the brogue, however, is the identification of the kinds of people most likely to speak it and to retain it as the region is transformed from a locally-based, marine economy to a more global, tourist-based economy, with all the social ramifications that go along with this change.*

In some communities once typified by their heavy use of the brogue, it may even be difficult for visitors to find people who speak it. This is certainly understandable, given the simple demographic statistics and dynamics of change. For example, consider the summertime statistics for an island like Ocracoke. During a typical summer day, anywhere from 3,000–5,000 people visit the island from the mainland, overwhelming the 600 permanent residents. At the same time, only about half of all the year-round residents are *ancestral islanders*, that is, people whose family genealogy is traceable to the island. To this equation, we must now add the fact that many younger residents no longer speak the brogue. The traditional dialect, then, might actually be found among less than three percent of the people on or around the island on any given day during the tourist season, and some of those people may be fishing in the sound or trying to stay out of harm's way. Visitors to Ocracoke or Hatteras in the summer months have often reported to me that they never heard the dialect we described in various books and articles. My advice to them is to go again during the off-season and search out a store or meeting place where locals congregate on a regular basis just to "say a word."

The situation is slightly different in a place like Harkers Island, where there are fewer *dingbatters* and *dit-dots,* and some of the younger local children are more likely to retain the brogue—at least until they attend high school on the mainland, where they have to make more linguistic choices about retaining their dialect in the face of majority pressure from their mainland peers. Even here, the strongest dialect speakers are likely to be those whose lives do not include everyday interaction with the visitors, and over half the people there during the summer are not locals by birth.

Although we might describe the typical speaker of the traditional brogue as an older lifetime resident of the Outer Banks who is connected to the marine-based culture (e.g., a fisherman or a boat builder), we have to be cautious about such a profile. The picture is really much more complex than that, and we have to be careful about stereotyping categories of classic speakers, such as the older, rugged fishermen with limited formal education and restricted contact with outsiders. For example, we know some middle-aged women who have a strong version of the brogue, and although younger speakers in general sound much less brogue-like than older Outer Banks residents, we have come across an occasional younger speaker who has chosen to maintain a strong version of the dialect.

*For a discussion of such changes, especially as they occur in maritime communities, see David Griffith's essay, "Coasts in the Works: Impressions of Working Waterfronts," in this volume, pp. 37–48.

The detailed study of different communities in coastal North Carolina has furthered our understanding that some patterns of brogue usage clearly do not match outside expectations. Some of the speakers who sound the most "brogue-ish" of all on Ocracoke are not the very oldest people; rather, they are a core group of middle-aged men who work and socialize together on a daily basis. Furthermore, this group includes a couple of men who were among the first college graduates of the island and even lived on the mainland for a period of time; so having a brogue is neither a simple matter of education nor even of continuous residency on the island. In this case, we found that the maintenance and intensification of the brogue by this group of speakers is probably related to the fact that the members of this group have a strong sense of island identity and are interested in maintaining certain traditional ways of life—including their dialect. We thus see that the brogue can sometimes be used symbolically to "make a statement" about being a part of the community culture and preserving certain forms of the traditional Outer Banks lifestyle.

Walt Wolfram laughs at an islander's joke.
(Image originally appeared in Wolfram and Schilling-Estes, *Hoi Toide on the Outer Banks*, pg. 51. Chapel Hill/London: UNC Press, 1997. Photo by Herman Lankford, courtesy of North Carolina Language and Life Project.)

Outsiders might also find it surprising that the brogue has been adopted by some African Americans on the Outer Banks as well, because people tend to associate it with Anglo-American rather than with African-American speech. However, we must remember that African Americans have been a part of coastal North Carolina for hundreds of years and have also participated in various activities related to coastal marine culture. For example, there were over 150 slaves who lived on Ocracoke and Portsmouth before the Civil War, and although they moved from Ocracoke to the mainland after 1865, they were probably exposed to the dialect. There have also been African Americans involved in fishing and a black lifesaving station on Pea Island on the Outer Banks (Weatherford).*

Both African Americans and Anglo Americans have lived in mainland Hyde County by the Pamlico Sound for almost three centuries. Early Anglo Americans inhabited mainland Hyde County in the first decade of the 1700s and shortly thereafter African Americans were brought from Maryland and Virginia. By the mid-1700s, approximately a third of the population was African American, and this ratio has been maintained through the centuries. In the two centuries of official census figures (1790–1990), the proportion of African Americans and Anglo Americans in Hyde County has remained much the same, with approximately one-third of the population being African American. Interviews with over 150 lifetime African-American residents of mainland Hyde County by the staff of the North Carolina Language and Life Project in the late 1990s reveal that many of the older African-American residents had quite strong versions of the brogue, including the traditional pronunciation of the *i* vowel of *tide*, the pronunciation of the

---

*For more information on African Americans on the North Carolina coast, see Walt Wolfram's essay, "African Americans by the Sea," in this volume, pp. 119–123.

ou vowel of *sound*, and the use of *weren't* in sentences such as *It weren't me*. Although our research (Wolfram, Thomas, and Green) shows that older African Americans also have retained some ethnically distinguishing dialect traits, we were impressed with the extensive adoption of brogue features by the older African-American speakers. In fact, when we play tape-recorded samples for listeners, we have found that they cannot reliably distinguish between some of the older African-American and Anglo-American speakers in mainland Hyde County.

We have also found that the brogue cuts across other social and religious lines that people might expect to be important. We already noted that the use of the brogue is not always distributed on the basis of level of education or occupation. In our study of the brogue on Harkers Island, we discovered that the presence of the brogue did not correlate neatly with significant religious divisions in the community. For example, Harkers Island has been the home of a significant congregation of the Church of Jesus Christ of Latter-day Saints (Mormons) for over a century now (Hancock), with a well-established church that stands apart from the various Protestant churches representing Methodists, Baptists, and Pentecostals on the island. Although we thought that dialect might correlate with religious affiliation, we did not find this to be the case. Even though the Mormon population may have come from Utah to this area later than some other groups, the long-term residency and association with the community resulted in the adoption of the same brogue that typifies other residents on Harkers Island.

The use of the brogue is most associated with long-term residency, lifestyle, and island identity. Some outsiders are good mimics and may pick up some of the words that are used in the local community. However, we have yet to find anyone who moved to this area whose speech precisely resembled the brogue of those long-time residents whose families have lived in the area for generations. At the same time, the changes that have overcome coastal North Carolina during the last half-century have clearly affected the brogue. Those strongly connected with the marine life of the area seem to be most likely to maintain the brogue as it becomes diluted with the economic and social transformation of the Outer Banks. Thus, fishermen, who spend a lot of time with each other on the water, are more likely to show a stronger version of the dialect than those who spend their everyday lives interacting with tourists. We have to be careful about such simple descriptions, though, because we have seen that dialect is also a matter of identity, and that those who wish to project their island heritage may maintain the brogue even in the face of extensive interaction with outsiders.

Where Did the Brogue Come From?

Given the uniqueness of the brogue among the dialects of American English, it is natural to ask where the brogue originated and how it developed over the centuries. The answer to this question is, however, somewhat complex in light of incomplete linguistic and historical documentation. We must therefore be content to speculate about its history based on various types of circumstantial historical and linguistic information. Our evidence includes an understanding of where the people migrated from and the dialect they brought with them, as well as a consideration of the development of the dialect over time.

To begin, we must recognize the *founder effect* in dialect development. This refers to the fact that the group introducing the language to the region originally will leave a lasting imprint on the linguistic heritage of the area. In this case, it means that the English dialect brought to the Outer Banks by the earliest groups of speakers who settled the area will still be reflected in the current population. Tracing this heritage is easier said than done, as there were different stages of "founding." Furthermore, all languages and dialects change continually regardless of social and historic circumstance—indeed, the only static language is a dead one. So we need to consider who brought the original language varieties to coastal Carolina and how the brogue might have evolved over the centuries.

When considering the founder effect on Outer Banks English, we need to consider several levels of influence. First, we must evaluate the contributions of different dialects from the British Isles to the dialect landscape of America. Then we need to think about the dialects of older American English, as the earliest permanent English settlers of the Outer Banks did not typically come directly from England. Finally, we need to consider the patterns of contact between Bankers and other groups over the centuries and how these might have affected the formation and subsequent development of the dialect.

Most of the early residents of the Outer Banks came south from Tidewater Virginia and from the eastern shores of Maryland. In fact, many residents of the region have family genealogies that trace their roots back to specific towns of origin in Virginia and Maryland, and some of these are even available on various Web sites (e.g., the Hyde County genealogy Web site at http://www.rootsweb.com/~nchyde/hyde.htm). Because most of the early migration south along the coast was by boat, there were few mainland roads and bridges spanning the complicated network of rivers, estuaries, inlets, and expansive marshlands. These geographical obstacles made overland travel impossible. The first order of dialect business, then, is to establish the kind of dialect that this group might have brought with them when they started migrating south by boat in the early and mid-1700s.

To get a picture of American English that pre-dated southern migration, we need to examine the dialects of the British Isles that might have been represented in coastal Virginia and Maryland. The inhabitants from the British Isles did not come from a single location, though certain regions of England may have been a more dominant influence than others (Fischer). For example, south-western England was well-represented in the early population, although there was certainly representation from East Anglia and other areas as well. The prominence of surnames like O'Neal and Scarborough to this day on the Outer Banks also suggests that an original Irish-English influence was part of the early dialect mix. We have already hinted at the possible affinity of Outer Banks English with some prominent features of Southwestern English in England, but there are also some features that can be traced to Irish English similar to those found in Appalachia, where the effect of Scots-Irish English is well-established (Montgomery).

Various dialects of the British Isles may have been represented among the early speakers in America, but the important point is that there was a selective process in the formative molding of a distinct dialect regionally associated with the coastal areas and islands of the Mid-Atlantic. What is most important about dialect traits such as the use of *weren't* for *wasn't* or the distinct pronunciation of *sound* is the fact that a population of speakers in a given area of America incorporated these features into their emerging dialect so that these features became associated with a distinct regional dialect of American English. Accordingly, we find the dialect birth of what became the coastal dialect that eventually diffused and developed into the Outer Banks dialect.

Obviously, the process of regional dialect development in English did not happen overnight, and dialectologists cannot pinpoint exactly when the Outer Banks dialect developed. One possibility is that the formative years of development took place during the early and mid-1700s, and those who migrated to the Outer Banks along the coast from Tidewater Virginia and coastal Maryland brought the basic version of the dialect with them. However, in *Tangier Island: Place, People, and Talk* (2000), David Shores takes the position that "the formative stages of these dialects [i.e., those of Chesapeake and Outer Banks island communities], that is, the period at which they took on the characteristics that they have today, would have been between 1800 and 1850, give or take a decade or two" (305). If Shores is right, then a lot of the Outer Banks dialect would have developed after the primary settlement had already taken place.

How would we then account for the strong resemblance between the Outer Banks dialects and island and coastal dialects to the north? We should remember that, to a large extent, the migration and movement of people on the Outer Banks was determined by the coastal waters, and that there is a history of movement up and down the waterways.[3] For example, at one point, the lower Outer Banks involved a whaling industry that connected with the whaling industry along the New England coast. We also know that many older men on Ocracoke even today spent time working in ports to the North, including those in Wilmington, Delaware, and Philadelphia, Pennsylvania. It is quite possible that continued movement up and down the coast after settlement might have led to the diffusion of dialect traits along the Mid-Atlantic coast. Although we cannot be certain about the time frame of the brogue's formative development, we know from our examination of written documents—such as the logs kept by lighthouse pilots, letters, and memoirs—that the dialect was well in place by the mid-1800s.

What Will Happen to the Brogue?

What is the future of the brogue? Is it dying? Will it survive the waves of *dingbatters* and *dit-dots* that have flooded the Outer Banks and have dramatically changed the economic and social complexion of those maritime communities during the last half-century? And does it make any difference if it dies? The classification of the brogue as an "endangered dialect" has sometimes caught the fancy of the media. For example, the Associated Press has circulated stories with headlines like "Ebb Tide on Hoi Toide" in prominent regional newspapers.

First, we must admit that the threat to the brogue in communities up and down coastal Carolina is very real. Some of the once-common traditional traits are vanishing rapidly. If we compare just three generations within the same family, we can see how quickly a unique language can die. In some families, the grandparents may still retain many traditional speech characteristics of the dialect, including the traditional pronunciation, vocabulary, and grammar. The children, however, show a significant reduction in the use of the forms, and the grandchildren have virtually none of these features. We have documented this pattern of dialect erosion in a number of families over the past decade, indicating that the dialect could, in fact, vanish in a couple of generations.

Certainly, dialectologists and linguists worry about the disappearance of the brogue, and liken language loss to the extinction of a biological species. People argue that these are not the same, and that people don't give up talking when a language dies; they just use another one. In fact, some individuals applaud language death and say that the reduction of the world's languages to just a few would make international communication much more efficient. Perhaps. It is also true that clothing manufacturing would be more efficient if we all wore the same kind and color of shirts or shoes, but where would that leave us in terms of expressing individual and cultural identity?

Dialectologists argue that science, culture, and history also perish when a language or dialect of a language dies. In the quest to understand the general nature of language, we learn from our differences, just as we learn about the general nature of life from biological diversity. For example, the observation of many different kinds of birds can teach us more about the aerodynamics of flight than would the observation of a single species limited to one size, weight, and skeletal structure. Similarly, studying varieties of English helps us understand the nature of our language and of language in general. That study is a worthy scientific and humanistic goal in itself as we seek—within our own particular disciplines—to gain a fuller understanding of the workings of the human mind.

When a language or dialect dies, an essential and unique part of human knowledge and culture dies with it. The Outer Banks would certainly still be the Outer Banks if the dialect were to disappear completely, but a cornerstone of traditional island culture surely would be lost if it did. I personally find it hard to imagine certain stories being told without the resonating sounds of the brogue. Similarly, I find it hard to imagine the same conversational effect taking place if words like "harassed," "visitor," or "upset in my stomach" were heard in place of *mommucked*, *dingbatter*, or *quamished in the gut*.

Even as we may mourn the seemingly inevitable passing of traditional dialect, we can be assured that people and their speech are dynamic and resilient, and that communities desiring to assert their uniqueness will find ways to do so, culturally and linguistically. We know of cases where communities have changed their overall manner of speaking but have consciously chosen new features of speech to continue to set them apart from others. For example, it may be that a couple of features of Outer Banks speech might be kept and redefined in terms of their symbolic significance, or that new features or words will be created to maintain dialect and community distinctiveness. Dialect distinctiveness in its traditional form is probably not a realistic option for the Outer Banks, but new creations—or the selective retention of a couple of the traditional ones—could perpetuate at least some dialect distinctiveness.

One thing seems to be certain about the brogue: since it has been an essential part of traditional Outer Banks culture, members of the communities and students in the schools need to know about the brogue if they want to maintain at least a semblance of their unique cultural legacy. The dialect heritage deserves to be indelibly documented and preserved—for *hoi toiders*, for new residents, and for tourists who wish to understand why the Banks and the people who inhabit them are so special.[4]

As a linguist and anthropologist, I believe that it would be an irrecoverable loss if the Outer Banks brogue died, but I have no say in such matters. The fate of the brogue is solely in the hands of the various coastal communities who will decide for themselves. However, all of us—especially islanders—should have a stake in ensuring that this tradition will be preserved.

Dave Esham of Ocracoke shares some island phrases with linguists Natalie Schilling-Estes and Walt Wolfram.

(Image originally appeared in Wolfram and Schilling-Estes, *Hoi Toide on the Outer Banks*, pg. 31. Photo by Herman Lankford, courtesy of North Carolina Language and Life Project.)

Wouldn't it be nice if the dialect traditions of the Outer Banks were documented as carefully as some of the genealogies that are being compiled to trace family heritage? A hundred years ago, we could only do that through written records, which wouldn't capture the flavor of the dialect. However, now all we have to do is turn on the video and audio recorder so that "young'uns" and the generations to come may share the sounds, stories, phrases, and observations of the people who for so long gave linguistic life to the Outer Banks. What a gift it would be if, a millennium from now, people could hear the sounds of the Outer Banks for themselves. Such an accomplishment was not possible when the English language developed a millennium ago, but we now have that potential. If nothing else, I hope we will not squander the opportunity to preserve and celebrate one of the greatest dialect traditions ever to develop in American society.

ENDNOTES

1. The irony of this episode was perhaps best highlighted by one of the Ocracokers who proceeded to read the passages in his version of a British accent rather than the Outer Banks dialect. I figured it was the television crew's just reward for their presumptuousness.

2. For example, Southern uses of words like carry ("take, accommodate"), cut off/on ("switch, turn off/on"), mash ("push"), kin ("relative"), and so forth are all quite common on the Outer Banks.

3. In addition to the well-known movement of trade and white migration up and down our eastern waterways, David S. Cecelski has recently written about the central role of African-American fishermen, harbor pilots, and other maritime workers—free and enslaved—along the southeastern Atlantic seaboard. See David S. Cecelski, *The Waterman's Song: Slavery and Freedom in Maritime North Carolina*. Chapel Hill/London: UNC Press, 2001.

4. To help achieve these ends, over the past decade the North Carolina Language and Life Project has conducted extensive recorded interviews with islanders of all ages. We have produced video documentaries, audio compact disks and cassettes, and a school-based curriculum for students to learn about their dialect heritage, and we have published numerous articles and two books documenting the Outer Banks dialect.

REFERENCES

Fischer, David Hackett. *Albion's Seed: Four British Folkways in America*. NY: Oxford Univ. Press, 1989.

Hancock, Joel G. *Strengthened by the Storm: The Coming of the Mormons to Harkers Island, N.C., 1897–1909*. Morehead City, NC: Campbell and Campbell, 1988.

Howren, Robert. "The Speech of Ocracoke, North Carolina." *American Speech* 37 (1962): 163–75.

Jaffe, Hilda. *The Speech of the Central Coast of North Carolina: The Carteret County Version of the Banks Brogue*. Publications of the American Dialect Society 60. Tuscaloosa: Univ. of Alabama Press, 1973.

Kay, Marvin L. and Lorin Lee Cary. *Slavery in North Carolina, 1748–1775*. Chapel Hill/London: UNC Press, 1995.

Montgomery, Michael. "Exploring the Roots of Appalachian English." *English World-Wide* 10 (1989): 227–78.

Shores, David. *Tangier Island: Place, People, and Talk*. Newark: Univ. of Delaware Press, 2000.

Weatherford, Carole Boston. *Sink or Swim: African-American Lifesavers of the Outer Banks*. Wilmington, NC: Coastal Carolina Press, 1999.

Wolfram, Walt and Natalie Schilling-Estes. *Hoi Toide on the Outer Banks: The Story of the Ocracoke Brogue*. Chapel Hill/London: UNC Press, 1997.

Wolfram, Walt, Kirk Hazen and Natalie Schilling-Estes. *Dialect Maintenance and Change on the Outer Banks*. Publications of the American Dialect Society 81. Tuscaloosa: Univ. of Alabama Press, 1999.

Wolfram, Walt, Erik Thomas and Elaine Green. "The Regional Context of Earlier African-American Speech: Reconstructing the Development of African-American Vernacular English." *Language in Society* 29 (2000): 315-45.

"Writing's the main thing"
Imaginative Coastal Literature for Young Readers

— James W. Clark, Jr. —

*I*f you want to write, come on over…Writing's the main thing" (Walser 202).

The young journalist to whom Paul Green sent this message in Oklahoma City in 1937 wanted to write plays. So he moved to North Carolina later that year, to live and work in Chapel Hill with the university close by and Green as a neighbor. Earning a degree in creative writing or drama was secondary to Noel Houston. Writing *was* his main thing.

Green completely understood and welcomed him into a writing group that met Sunday evenings that winter in Green's living room. Houston flourished in this rich environment and soon completed several new plays about Oklahoma.

Recently, Green had been absorbed in the pre-colonial history of his own native state. His symphonic drama *The Lost Colony* had just run from Independence Day through Labor Day, 1937, at the Waterside Theater in Manteo. On this same site Sir Walter Raleigh's colonists of 1587 had begun their long, speculative journey into imaginative literature by disappearing into history. Where did they go? Why? When? How?

President Franklin Roosevelt attended a special performance of *The Lost Colony* August 18, 1937. From his car parked high in the amphitheater, the President spoke to the large audience. Beyond them, roughly ten nautical miles across Roanoke Sound, he could see at Kill Devil Hills the 1932 granite monument commemorating the Wright brothers' first manned flight in December 1903. After praising Green's dynamic symphonic drama, Roosevelt noted that the immediate occasion for his visit to this historic region of North Carolina was the 350th birthday of Virginia Dare, believed to be the first English child born in the New World.

Both before and after Paul Green, North Carolina writers have contemplated the fate of this infant and the other colonists. An early example is Greenville's Sallie Southall Cotton, who in 1901 published a long narrative poem entitled, *The White Doe: The Fate of Virginia Dare, An Indian Legend*. In 1988, William H. Hooks, a native of Columbus County, added to his impressive list of books for young readers *The Legend of the White Doe*, a work of historical fiction. And most recently, *Pale as the Moon* (1999), Donna Campbell's young adult novel about a

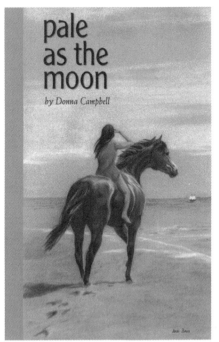

pale
as the
moon
by Donna Campbell

Native American girl, presents a new interpretation of the misty facts surrounding the Roanoke colonists. Over water and land, the girl leads her English friends to safety on the mainland, even as her own people are preparing to attack the island settlement.

In Act I of Paul Green's *The Lost Colony*, the pregnant Eleanor Dare, still waiting in England to set sail, declares before Queen Elizabeth I in a strong, fresh voice: "If England's men have dreams, so have her women" (17). These bold but ill-fated adventurers motivated, Green believed, by the dream of founding a democratic society, passed down a demanding legacy to others, including himself and his contemporaries. He and many of them who lived by this dream could already see in Hitler's Nazi tactics the beginnings of another world war.

Noel Houston saw this threat. He also saw *The Lost Colony* in 1938, during his first of many summer vacations on the North Carolina coast at Nags Head and Roanoke Island. He absorbed local history and lore, such as the legend of the white doe, and began to feel like a Tar Heel. He observed the coastal blackouts under worsening military conditions during the summer of 1942, as more than seventy-five tankers and cargo ships were torpedoed just offshore by German U-boats. Meanwhile, his literary passion turned from drama toward prose fiction after a very timely story exploded in his imagination. On May 8, 1943, he published "Lantern on the Beach." In *Short Stories from the Old North State* (1959), Richard Walser later preserved this seminal work as a memorial to Houston, who had died in 1958.

Houston's tale is about young Eddie Daniel, age twelve. Eddie lives on the Outer Banks with his mother, a Red Cross worker, and his father, who tends the drawbridge to Roanoke Island. His sister is employed in a Norfolk munitions factory. Idly kicking the sand, Eddie feels useless—even angry. There's nothing for a boy his age to do. Within twenty-four hours, however, he has become a local hero. Eddie's older brother, Harvey, is burned to death when a German submarine, three miles offshore, blows up his tanker. That night, recalling and reenacting the land-pirate legend of how Nags Head got its name, Eddie ties a lantern around the neck of his pony,* Tuney, and lures the enemy sub into the breakers. It is destroyed on the beach, and the Coast Guard captures its crew.

Eddie learned this Nags Head legend from Old Man Si Denning. Truly the boy's spiritual grandfather and consoling friend, Si builds castles of mere words and lives in a one-room shack surrounded by salt grass tufts. Most of his oral tales concern the Outer Banks, but one, like Eddie's own desire to find his place in the war effort, is personal. As a young man, Si was among the

---

*For more information on horses of the Outer Banks, see Carmine Prioli's essay, "The Wild Horses of Shackleford Banks," in this volume, pp. 138–141.

natives Orville and Wilbur Wright enlisted at Kitty Hawk in 1903 to run alongside and steady their flying machine. As the craft rose in the air, Si's left forefinger snagged between two wires and a piece was yanked off. Rubbing the remaining stump, the Old Man proudly showed Eddie the results of the world's very first "airyplane" accident.

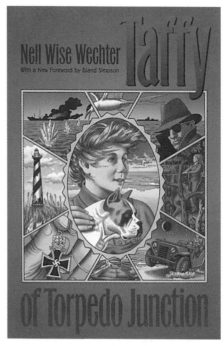

Paul Green's *The Lost Colony* regained its early fame through annual summer performances after the blackout years of World War II. It remains a popular educational and entertainment resource for youth and adults alike, while Houston's "Lantern on the Beach," the apprenticeship story that made him a North Carolinian, lies buried. Yet in this literary treasure chest are virtually all of the elements to be found in a selection of the state's imaginative coastal writing for young people since the 1930s.

What are these elements? They include: the ocean and its coastal communities in time of crisis, whether a war or a fierce storm; young people in relation to themselves and others, especially old men; the mysteries of being about twelve years old; and the varied roles of available family members. Animals, tame and wild, also figure prominently in these works. Finally, stories to live by are vital to Eddie's survival and growth in "Lantern on the Beach" and in these other selected titles. First are *Taffy of Torpedo Junction* (1957) by Nell Wise Wechter and *The Old Man and the Boy* (1957) by Robert Ruark, both well known. Then comes James R. Hurst's "The Scarlet Ibis" (1960), anthologized in Scott Foresman's *Patterns in Literature* (1985). *Stranger from the Sea: Teetoncey* (1974), Theodore Taylor's first "Outer Banks Trilogy" book, and Nancy Tilly's splendid *Golden Girl* (1985) follow. *Sound the Jubilee* (1995), a Civil War tale about Roanoke Island by Sandra Forrester, and *Bear at the Beach* (1996), Clay Carmichael's fable of finding a home at the edge of the sea, complete the survey. *The Lost Colony* (1937) and "Lantern on the Beach" (1943) form one bookend for this collection. The other is provided by the five books of coastal lore and legend written by Charles Harry Whedbee: *Legends of the Outer Banks and Tar Heel Tidewater* (1966), *The Flaming Ship of Ocracoke and Other Tales of the Outer Banks* (1971), *Outer Banks Mysteries & Seaside Stories* (1978), *Outer Banks Tales to Remember* (1985) and *Black-beard's Cup and Stories of the Outer Banks* (1989). In each of these collections, Whedbee provides fascinating tales like the ones Nell Wise Wechter and Noel Houston, with similar motivations, had already discovered on their own.

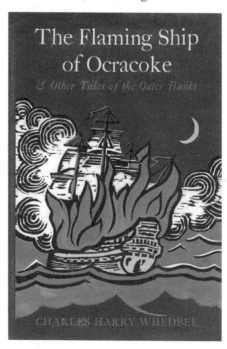

Their young characters, Taffy Willis and Eddie Daniel, also share many characteristics. Taffy and Daniel are a World War II heroine and hero who live on the Outer Banks, she at Cape Hatteras (or Torpedo Junction) and he at Nags Head. Both know about wartime blackouts, and both are devoted to animals. Aided by his pony and armed with the old legend, Eddie cleverly destroys a German submarine. Taffy, a year older, mixes keen observations with other clues and, amid great danger, employs her pony and a dog she rescued from the surf to enable authorities to capture on-shore saboteurs from Baltimore who are collaborating with the German U-boat crews. Both youth know the Atlantic. Taffy loves and respects the ocean, but does not fear it, even though those perilous waters drowned both of her parents when she was just three years old. Eddie, who witnessed the death of his badly-burned brother, Harvey, on the beach, senses that the ocean will get him, too, if he turns his back on it. Still, he uses his special knowledge of the coast to avenge Harvey's murder by the Germans.

Eddie is bonded to Old Man Si Denning, more than to his mother and father with whom he lives. Gramp Morgan is Taffy's only family, and she adores him and the old fishing shack they share on the point of the Cape, even if some folks say an old man ought not to raise a young girl. Gramp is stocked full of the Bible and its lessons to live by, while Old Man Si Denning has obviously drilled coastal lore and legends into young Eddie. In many respects Wechter and Houston tell the same story, one about a girl, the other about a boy.

In Robert Ruark's *The Old Man and the Boy*, a grandfather named Ned takes his grandson to raise. The boy lives mainly with his parents, but on weekends, summers, holidays, and hooky days, the two are virtually inseparable as they hunt, fish, talk, travel, and eat. Miss Lottie, the grandmother, suffers insults and slights but maintains control as the game is harvested and prepared or preserved. In fact, respect for wildlife and a love of dogs that hunt well permeate the novel. The boy's later success in the Navy during World War II is based upon learning about land and sea, as well as upon good books from such a devoted but testy teacher as the Old Man. To prove the boy was worthy to have a horse, the Old Man made him tame and tend a goat. By then, he had already learned to kill or catch deer, squirrels, birds, geese, ducks, and fish. The boy becomes a hunting hero for not giving in to his youthful urge to kill all of the fowl in the field or on the water. His is a war within. He wins that one and, to his own benefit and his grandfather's pleasure, he mixes well with the local races and creeds.

Old Man Ned is a salty naturalist who has spent most of his life on the water. Almost always, he philosophizes to the point of stretching his facts. The boy knows that each telling, however exaggerated, is aimed at the marrow of his own being. His deep love allows his first-person narrative to glide good-naturedly through his boyhood in a belated tribute to his Old Man. That the boy masters the lessons and a genuine style is clear:

> What I can remember best is the ghostly cold of a predawn sailing, the clammy dew on the tarpaulins—dew stiff-bristled on the hempen lines, cold-flecked on the deck, smeared across the glass of the bridge. I can remember the crash of the sea against ship, the tremor all the way along her as she took a big one, the way anything that wasn't battened down took a walk when the seas were on the beam, and the crashing in the galleys and the cursing of the cook and the smell of coffee grounds frying when the coffee pot up-ended on the galley stove.

I remember the bone-crushing fatigue at the end of the day, when you came bravely into port with your full-up flags flying, and the sun going down red, and the night chill coming on again. And the way the dock pitched when you tied up and your sea-limber legs hit firm planking again, and still continued to roll and pitch with the motion of the sea.

I saw an albatross before I read *The Ancient Mariner*, and what is more, I knew a boat that was named after one. I knew about the hunter home from the hills, and the sailor home from the sea (269).

In the old men who nurture them, Eddie Daniel and Taffy Willis are not more fortunate than Robert Ruark's well-made boy from the coastal area of southeastern North Carolina.

James R. Hurst grew up in tiny Marines, North Carolina, north of Wilmington and south of Cape Hatteras and Nags Head. Once a jumping-off place for anglers and duck hunters in Onslow County, this coastal paradise on the New River was demolished so that Camp Lejeune could be built early in World War II. "The Scarlet Ibis" is Hurst's poignant story about the place he had known as a boy. His chief characters are two boys, one of whom, the twelve-year-old, grows up and looks back at boyhood. His story, like *The Old Man and the Boy*, is a first-person narrative. The subject is Doodle, the narrator's long-dead brother, whom he remembers having been ashamed of when they were boys. Doodle—his real name was William Armstrong—was a weakling born in a caul. Their maid, Aunt Nicey, said this membrane—made from "the nightgown of Jesus"—was a sign the baby would live. Somehow, Doodle does live, though he has a big head and crawls backward. His tiny body is red and as shriveled as an old man's. He cannot walk. He becomes an embarrassment to his older brother at home and—because he survives long enough to be enrolled there—embarrasses him at school, too. Still, a brotherly relationship eventually develops.

Doodle clings to the older boy, who, in turn, is sometimes kind, as when he takes Doodle to see the natural beauty of Old Woman Swamp. On another day, they climb up to the barn loft where Doodle is shown the mahogany coffin their father had made for the sickly child. He is made to touch it. As he does, a screech owl flaps out of the box into their faces. Doodle is motionless and cries: "Don't leave me. Don't leave me" (53).

At age five, Doodle gets walking lessons during the summer from his determined brother in the sanctuary of Old Woman Swamp. Doodle would rather make honeysuckle wreaths, but one day he does walk. The next day, he takes a few more unsupported steps. His astonished parents witness this miracle for the first time on his sixth birthday in early October. Although pride alone—to avoid the public shame of having a crippled brother—has motivated the older boy, his success in teaching Doodle to walk bonds them more closely than ever. So Doodle reciprocates. He teaches his brother to lie; and he, to repay him, decides to teach Doodle to row, run, swim, climb trees, and fight!

During the summer of 1918 they make some progress, but nature itself seems to have turned against all humanity that year. The world is at war. Scalding drought in May and June is followed in July by a blasting hurricane from the east. It ruins the family's cotton and corn crops; in the boys' stunned presence their daunted father curses "heaven, hell, the weather, and the Republican Party" (56). On the horizon, meanwhile, looms Doodle's first day of school, but in the eyes of his demanding brother, Doodle is not yet physically ready.

One Saturday during family lunch, another storm, this one from the south, blows a loudly croaking, worn-out red bird into the bleeding tree in the yard. Doodle tenderly identifies with this fowl that soon falls dead from its branch into the grass. Taking care to avoid germs and singing "Shall We Gather at the River" very softly, Doodle proceeds to the front flower garden and beside the petunias he buries this creature his daddy calls a scarlet ibis.

Soon the red, bedraggled Doodle is dead, too. For later that same afternoon, as yet another storm is brewing, he is exhorted by his brother beyond all limits to row against the tide back to Horseshoe Landing. This storm leaves both boys—one living, one dead—drenched in rain, blood, and tears.

As fierce as any military undertaking or destructive storms from the sea is the costly war against pride in this coastal story of two brothers, the sensitive weakling and his prideful boss. This older boy is too young, however, and cannot then manifest the sustaining love of the old men in the works by Houston, Wechter, and Ruark. For Hurst's narrator this maturity arrives with the years, and this stunning narrative becomes a memorial to the older brother as well as to Doodle. In time, the survivor has found in himself the expressive charm of the dead child's sensitive and loving soul. In fact, no reader can doubt that ultimately these two brothers have come together to make another wonderful, older man—the narrator of "The Scarlet Ibis."

Not two brothers, but twelve-year-old Ben O'Neal and a shipwrecked girl of the same age form the human core of Theodore Taylor's *Stranger from the Sea: Teetoncey*. This novel, set in 1898 on the coast between Cape Hatteras and Rodanthe, is ultimately as rough and tough as Hurst's story of Doodle is tender. By the time a hairpin-shaped, mute girl washes ashore from the wreck of the *Malta Express*, young Ben has already lost his daddy, John, a surfman, to the ocean and his brother, Guthrie, to Pamlico Sound. An older brother, Reuben, is working as second mate on a coastal brig, and Ben, having completed all of the schooling a boy could get on the Banks, wants to go to sea too. But his mother, Rachel, holds him back, and not for the first time either. When he was born and for some time thereafter, she viewed Ben as her female child. Now she wants him to be less rough and daring than his father had been. The men on the coast (including Filene Midgett, Keeper of Heron Head Lifesaving Station) know that Rachel's last boy had been raised as a girl until the age of five. Rather than being grandfathers or surrogate fathers, the men view Ben as probably ruined for work like theirs and his late father's. By taking a major role in the rescue of the small and fragile girl Mr. Midgett names "Teetoncey," Ben begins to build a reputation as a worthy boy among these older men. Helping his mother care for their frail and silent houseguest teaches Ben to be the attentive son his mother now wants. And, of course, the girl is Rachel's long-awaited daughter. Ben cries tears of joy when Teetoncey regains her ability to speak and can thank him for his help and his acceptance.

Whereas Doodle dies at the end of Hurst's coastal story, Tee is alive and happy, no longer handicapped, in the last chapter of Taylor's novel. This accomplishment has made Ben, once considered a sissy by men and too rough by his mother, into a young man with healthy emotions and a new sister.

Skeptical neighbors, old and young, are helpful in the gradual process of remaking this single-parent, coastal family, but the natural environment is especially important. The raging Atlantic awakens Teetoncey from her muteness when Ben, at Rachel's request, takes the girl during a subsequent night storm to visit the beach where she had been rescued. A scream like nothing Ben has ever heard knifes out of Tee's knotted face. Both of her parents drowned the night the *Malta Express* broke up right offshore. Ben understands. Moreover, Ben's pet, Boo Dog, accepts the stranger from the sea as does his pony, Fid. Even the migratory snow geese on Pea Island help Tee feel more alive before she regains her voice and strength. Ben, too, is brought to his senses when a sudden storm on the sound flips over his small Creef boat and nearly drowns him in the icy water.

Three essential cultural features of *Stranger from the Sea: Teetoncey* both distinguish Taylor's novel and reveal its realism, its own rough readiness that persists despite Ben's new sensibilities. First, the ocean itself is an insult. It spits in people's eyes. The manly surfmen are deathly afraid of the ocean. Keeper Midgett damns it without ever cussing. Rachel, a native of the Outer Banks and a lifelong dune resident, thoroughly hates the Atlantic and will not go down to it or even look its way. While not blind to the rugged beauty of her surroundings and aware of occasional feelings of great contentment and peace, she damns the Yankee soldiers who had cut down all of the trees on the sound side during the Civil War. As a result, she figures, the blowing sand will shove every Banker into the sound if the fierce tides do not do it first. *"The sea giveth and the sea taketh away…"* is her philosophy (49). If she were not a woman she would "curse the sea all the way back to Noah's Ark" (32).

The novel's second cultural feature is revealed in the efforts Ben and Rachel make to introduce Tee to her new environment, which is similar to the one Taffy Willis will thrive in as an ocean orphan a few decades later. Shipwrecks, old and new, famous storms, and the Hatteras Lighthouse, that two-hundred-seven-foot echo chamber with two hundred sixty-eight steps, are examples of some similarities. En route to Pea Island to see the snow geese, Ben tells Tee about John White, Virginia Dare, and the lost colony of Roanoke Island. Earlier, at his mother's direction, he told her about the whalebone fences around some local houses and the early Hatterask and Poteskeets Indians. Ben brags to Tee that Blackbeard had been beheaded by Captain Maynard not thirty miles from their own dock and that the Union iron-clad *Monitor* had foundered off Cape Hatteras during the Civil War. He knows these stories from hearing his mother and other adults tell them all of his life. Like Eddie Daniel in "Lantern on the Beach," Ben wants to put the tales to immediate use, not to exact revenge from a wartime enemy but to revive Tee from the trauma of her shipwreck.

Actually, Ben's mother has proudly told him another version of the Nags Head story that Old Man Si Denning would later tell Eddie. Rachel believes she knows what is legend and what is outright lie or truth:

> Even though there was a place below Jockey Ridge named Nag's Head, which supposedly got its title from the lantern-toting ponies, not a word of truth was in the land-pirate story. The men would double over when they heard it. Anyone in their right mind who wanted to lure a ship ashore would put the pony on the beach, not inland on Jock Ridge (48).

To her the whole land-pirate thing is a dedicated lie that got started more than a century before. After all, she says, most of the old folks had become Bankers by surviving shipwrecks themselves.

The third cultural feature of Taylor's work is its detailed attention to the language of Rachel, Ben, and their neighbors. "Teetoncey" is Filene Midgett's pronunciation of *teetincy.* More than Houston or Wechter, both of whom employ "hoi toider"* speech in their characterizations, Taylor, who was born in Statesville but spent time as a child and as an adult on the coastal plain, collected vocabulary and ascribed it, through a British professor, to Devon. Indeed, many of Raleigh's lost colonists of 1587 came from that part of England. Ben's Fid, the pony, is a *tackie.*** Rachel's herbal medicines are *penetrates.* Tee's mind has been *mommicked* (in popular usage, also 'mommucked') or fouled-up. Something ruined is *berlask.* Before Tee can speak and Ben discovers that she is really Wendy Lynn Appleton from London, Ben introduces her to other words in his Banker vocabulary from Devon to see if she will recognize any of them: *fleech* ("to flatter"), *couthy* ("capable"), *mindable* ("paying attention"), *studiments* ("lessons"), and *swayzed* ("moved around") (78). This vivid linguistic detail balances Taylor's equally realistic and picturesque exposition:

> The islands stretched like a thin, drawn hunter's bow for a hundred seventy-five miles from up around Knott's Island, near the Virginia border, down to Cape Lookout, cutting sharp west at Hatteras Lighthouse and the vicious Diamond sand bars. Over the years surging seas cut new inlets, and new islands would be born. Then the sea and sand would fill in, closing the inlets (3).

Golden Girl by Nancy Tilly of Chapel Hill is set in Kingsport, a coastal town like Beaufort near Cape Lookout. The novel's Davis City would be Morehead City on a map of North Carolina, just as New Basil is situated inland about where New Bern can be found. Yet coastal geography is not nearly as important in this work as personal geography. Where does Penny Askew fit in—at home and in her crowd—as she enters junior high school? The inlet waters for sailing, the local library, Carrot Island with its feral horses, and certain people in the old town, including family and friends old and new, combine forces to bring her eventually to "golden girl" status. It is not easy. Yet she is capable and dying to write about horses if only she can find the time—and her lost manuscript. Her speech is not grammatical, and her hair needs fixing.

Penny's family, despite her mother's inertia and eventual surgery, is intact and more functional than the families of her female friends. In Henry Morgan she has a reliable boy her age to befriend, whether they are sailing his boat, the *Penny Ante,* or meeting at the library. Young love is not seriously mixed up in their good relationship. Like the boy in Ruark's novel, these two are also readers who dream of writing as well as they can sail. They win a race, beating Jack Bloodworth and his dad; Penny gets the third-prize ribbon in a literary contest. And finally Jack asks Penny out for dates.

---

*For more on the Outer Banks dialect, see Walt Wolfram's essay, "Speech at the Beach: The Outer Banks Brogue," in this volume, pp. 9–21.

**The term "tackie" or "marsh tackie" is one of several popular designations for the feral horses that for generations have roamed the sea islands off the coasts of Virginia, North Carolina, and Georgia. "Tackie" is believed to derive from the way tacky mud from the marshes stick to their feet. Elsewhere, the horses are known as marsh, Banks, or sand ponies.

Old friend Tracey Bingham, feeling unloved and destructive at home and away, and Margaret Draper, pretty and rich, provide along with other small-town youth a varied gathering not found in other juvenile works about the coast. When these two girls pressure Penny to join them into stealing something from Bynum's for the fun of it, she goes along. But Penny alone takes the time to confess to her parents, return the stolen lip pencil to the store with an apology, and, finally, take the heat from Tracey and Margaret when her father tells their fathers what has happened. She endures without feeling superior, and she takes up for Tracey in particular, even when Tracey is at her worst. Mr. Bingham threatens to punish Tracey by selling her horse, Thor. He relents, but the horse novel his wayward daughter and Penny had planned to write together is left up in the air. Yet the ending Penny creates for the rewritten horse story she completes for the contest is a hopeful sign. She calls the piece "Wild Horses." In it, Olivia decides that her love for King, her favorite stallion, requires her to overcome her own selfishness and leave him to run wild on his island by the sea.

Imagine Henry Morgan and Penny Askew sailing out of the fiction of Kingsport Inlet into the reality of Beaufort Inlet today. Now adults, these old friends could hardly be expected to avoid the site where in November 1996, almost exactly two hundred seventy-eight years to the day since Captain Maynard killed Blackbeard in Ocracoke Inlet, the wreck of the infamous pirate's former flagship, *Queen Anne's Revenge*, was discovered two miles from shore. What would Henry and Penny find to admire in Blackbeard or his stolen ship? Would they be amazed to hear that local educators invite their students to dress as Blackbeard—alias Edward Teach— and come to school in honor of this pirate and his sorry history? Henry might ask: What good character values does a grand rascal exhibit? And what, Penny might wonder, is the quality of any coastal tourism generated by the exhibition of artifacts harvested from the drowned remains of this thief's *Queen Anne's Revenge*? Of course, they both know that the Blackbeard legend has always been powerful, if not appealing. Richard Walser and Nancy Roberts, among numerous other North Carolina writers, have enhanced Teach's durable and dubious celebrity. And to date, *Queen Anne's Revenge* is North Carolina's oldest identified shipwreck. Along the Graveyard of the Atlantic, that is a worthwhile distinction.

But a writer as honest as Penny Askew, with a critic as steady as Henry, could lead young readers to consign Blackbeard's manner of wildness to its proper offshore oblivion. Rather than feature the rapacious pirate, Penny's new coastal novel could focus on Hugh Williamson, a truly great North Carolinian. Williamson's mother, Mary Davison, was captured at age three by this feared pirate. In fact, she probably endured her brief captivity on board this same *Queen Anne's Revenge*, and then was released unharmed to complete her family's voyage from Ireland to Pennsylvania. If Blackbeard or his men had killed the young Mary Davison in 1718, she would not have grown up to marry John W. Williamson of Chester County and later give birth to Hugh and his nine brothers and sisters.

Eventually, Hugh settled in Edenton, North Carolina, and supported the Revolutionary War effort there by funding a tannery. In Winton, he developed a shipbuilding operation. Hugh Williamson also ran a mercantile business and practiced medicine. Befriended by Governor Richard Caswell, he was selected to vaccinate North Carolina's troops against smallpox at New

Bern. Soon he was the state's surgeon general. During the August 1780 Battle of Camden, he cared for Americans held prisoner behind enemy lines and later that year conducted dietary, sanitary, and clothing experiments with soldiers quartered in the Great Dismal Swamp. Records suggest that he advanced his own funds to support this work. Only two men died and just one went on sick leave that winter.

This real hero, whom Blackbeard could have erased from history, also won political office. He was elected from Edenton to the North Carolina House of Commons in 1782. In eleven years of continuous service, he represented the state in New York, Philadelphia, and Annapolis. He signed the U.S. Constitution for North Carolina and worked hard for its ratification. The list of Hugh Williamson's positive accomplishments goes on and on. Penny Askew's novel about this worthy public servant would provide young readers in the new century and millennium with a way to put wild Blackbeard in perspective. Williamson's stark contrast to Blackbeard might even inspire some boys and girls to write belated letters to Blackbeard's mother. For example, someone could let her know about her son, sweet little Eddie, who went from good to bad and worse: "Dear Mrs. Teach, I am sorry to tell you that…" Such letters would be purely imaginative exercises, but like all fiction based on fact, they could have potentially positive effects on young writers as well as readers. Of course, Mary Davison Williamson deserves some letters from Tar Heel boys and girls too. "Dear Mary, Do you know about how great your son Hugh became? He…" If such a work of fiction about Edward Teach and Hugh Williamson can inspire middle schoolers or younger boys and girls to compose letters to Mrs. Teach and Mrs. Williamson, Penny's career as a young adult novelist will have set sail in the right direction. And it will introduce a whole generation of young writers to the wisdom of Paul Green's directive that "Writing's the main thing."

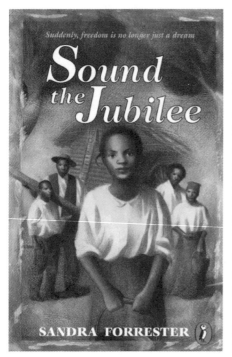

This speculative effort to direct attention from one personality or epoch to another is in keeping with the fiction of Durham's Sandra Forrester. She researched, wrote, and published *Sound the Jubilee* (1995) in an effort to focus on the Civil War history of Roanoke Island, a place already staked out by Paul Green and others to commemorate the dramatic story of English colonists lost long ago. Forrester's story is about a spunky slave girl named Maddie. She comes with her family from a mainland plantation to Nags Head to humor their white mistress as the Yankees close in on North Carolina. After Union forces capture Roanoke Island, with her literate family and several thousand other former but illiterate slaves, Maddie inhabits the northern part of the island between January 1862 and the end of the War Between the States. Work for pay is promised to the men. Women and girls volunteer in the camp hospital and maintain a tent encampment.

Maddie, for her part, mainly teaches the children and some adults to read and write. She struggles to convince her friend, Zebedee, to join her class. For this important work, one Christmas a Sergeant Taylor gives her a copy of Walt Whitman's *Leaves of Grass*. Portions of this text become Maddie's story of freedom to live by, and her father, Titus, loves for her to read aloud Whitman's song about the open road. Her father wants his freedom. To this end Titus and his maturing daughter also have a special, uniquely coastal treasure:

> Maddie followed his gaze to the east, where the sky was alive with hundreds of beating wings. The birds were white, with black-tipped wings.
> She came over to stand by Titus. He placed an arm around her shoulder. "What are they, Papa?"
> "Snow geese." Royall had come out of his tent. He walked over to join them. "Comes down from Canada this time ever' year. Spends the winter over on Pea Island."
> "Snow geese," Maddie repeated. "That's a beautiful name."
> "Suits 'em," Titus said.
> "Think how much'a the world they see," Maddie said. She didn't know where this place called Canada was, but it must be far away from North Carolina. "Wouldn't it be nice to fly anywhere you wanted to?"
> "It shorely would be," Titus agreed. "Many's a day I envied the birds, with the whole sky their home" (110–11).

Soon Titus and Royall, who is engaged to Maddie's sister, join the Union Army. The last night Titus spends with his family, now living in a new log house they have built on Roanoke Island, he strokes Maddie's head and asks her to read Whitman's poem of the open road. She complies. Then he tells her to go on reading Whitman aloud on future nights just as if he were still there. "Wherever I am, I'll hear you, Maddie. You just go on readin' and I'll hear" (130).

When Royall's leg is shattered in battle, he returns to the island to recover and to get married. Titus does not return. He is killed and buried in Tennessee, four months before the family gets the news. Maddie, by then an assistant to Miss James, a white teacher sent from up North to the local school, cannot read Whitman or grieve for her father because of "a roaring in her head— like the waves hitting the beach at Nags Head—and she felt like she was drowning" (166).

But that October the snow geese fly back to Pea Island:

> Maddie stood with her head thrown back, eyes shaded by her hand, watching their graceful flight. She was lost in the memory of one autumn morning when she and Titus had stood outside their tent enjoying the sight of a thousand such birds soaring across the sky. The stone in her chest shifted. Suddenly she felt the most searing pain she had ever known. And the tears that had refused to come were welling up in her eyes, blurring the image of the birds, pouring down her cheeks like salty rivers (171).

Brave Maddie cries out in hurt surprise, like Tee's sharp scream when Ben brought her back to the site of her rescue. Soon Miss James comes to Maddie and silently assists her in preparing a symbolic grave for Titus on Roanoke Island. Maddie has finally told her beloved papa goodbye. As her family moves to the mainland after the end of the Civil War, Maddie reads his favorite passage from Whitman, and she wonders if Papa hears:

Allons! The inducements will be greater,
We will sail pathless and wild seas,
We will go where winds blow, waves dash, and
the Yankee clipper speeds by under full sail (183).

After her family is settled on a new farm, Maddie wants to fly away North.

The bear in Clay Carmichael's *Bear at the Beach* (1996) is also searching for a father and a home. He lives with Clara, who tries to comfort him during his coastal search. Messages on paper ships in the outgoing tide bring no responses. The sea and the fish are not able to help the fatherless bear. Ducks also fail him when he asks for their help. A clam can't help either. Then a boy building a castle on the beach suggests that the bear build himself a father out of sand. He does, and the tide that washes his masterpiece out to sea makes him cry. Bear's journey toward home finally ends satisfactorily when he realizes, in conversation with a hermit crab and then with his friend Clara, that home is where you are safe and cared for and loved.

This lucky bear's condition and environment resonate well with the lives of the young human characters in these imaginative coastal writings. To him as to Maddie, Penny, Taffy, Ben, Eddie, and the others, the ocean and its North Carolina beaches both give and take away. The tides go out. They also reach inland, into hearts and minds, with hurt as well as consolation. Not pirate booty buried somewhere in the sand, but these stories to live by are the coastal treasure young readers can discover. Here are sturdy characters, young and old, who suggest whom we have been and whom we are becoming. The works especially show how to survive the winds and storm surges of adolescence, while gaining respect for each other and a deep love of coastal ecology.

The Cape Hatteras Lighthouse now stands magnificently and safely on its new ground near the sea. In one sense, these writings are even mightier than this black and white candy-striped beacon. Modern seafaring technology has made our beloved lighthouse obsolete, yet the famous landmark has been deservedly saved, embraced as a symbol of coastal heritage—of strength, hope, hazard, and home. By contrast, these timely coastal North Carolina stories are still marks to steer by—from the freedom dreams of Paul Green's Roanoke colonists to those of Maddie and her papa in *Sound the Jubilee*.

REFERENCES

Forrester, Sandra. *Sound the Jubilee*. NY: Penguin, 1955.

Green, Paul. *The Lost Colony: A Symphonic Drama of Man's Faith and Work*. Durham, NC: Seeman, 1980.

Hurst, James. "The Scarlet Ibis." In *Patterns in Literature*. 7th ed. Edited by Edmund J. Farrell et al. Glenville, IL: Scott Foresman, 1985.

Ruark, Robert. *The Old Man and the Boy*. NY: Henry Holt, 1957.

Taylor, Theodore. *Stranger from the Sea: Teetoncey*. NY: Avon, 1974.

Walser, Richard, ed. *Short Stories from the Old North State*. Chapel Hill, NC: UNC Press, 1959.

Coasts in the Works
Impressions of Working Waterfronts

— David Griffith —

Thomas Jefferson once noted that watermen were ahead of the scholars of his day by naming a common coastal phenomenon of light and distance, where objects on the horizon appeared larger, not smaller, than they actually were. In Yorktown, he mistook a canoe containing three men for a ship with three masts. "The seamen call it *looming*," Jefferson wrote. And he further declared: "Philosophy is as yet in rear of the seamen, for so far from having accounted for it, she has not given it a name" (Jefferson 120).

This paradox—the relative sluggishness of formally educated minds to understand or even name natural phenomena that common folk have already assimilated—may be less remarkable than one might think. Close observation of one's surroundings, from fishing, hunting, or other regular interaction with nature, often yields insights that predate scientific discovery. Emerson anticipated many of the principles of ecology by a little over a century in his 1847 poem entitled "Each and All," chronicling the loss of beauty that occurs when one removes things from their natural habitats. "All are needed," he wrote, "by each one; Nothing is good or fair alone" (Emerson 9). Henry David Thoreau, one of our first and most famous environmentalists, also embraced Emerson's idea.

Of course, Emerson and Thoreau were educated men. They were not of the same social class as the seamen whom Jefferson was talking about. Yet Emerson, Thoreau, and Jefferson's seamen shared powers of human observation largely unfettered by scientific models and specialties. In *Beautiful Swimmers: Watermen, Crabs and the Chesapeake Bay* (1976), William W. Warner comments upon the same trait. He observes that local watermen had discovered several characteristics of crabs long before marine biologists even considered studying them. At the bottom of these discoveries is the human mind's mysterious ability to process and combine several sets of stimuli simultaneously, to allow for incomplete information and imprecise measurement, to mix immediate sensory perception with experience, memory, history, heritage, and pride.

In the case of watermen, such discoveries draw upon repeated observations based on the accumulated knowledge of countless nautical forays under a variety of conditions. Fishing

excursions are often highly experimental, blending a lifetime of practical knowledge with immediate observations from the deck of a moving vessel. As such, they share certain characteristics
with the practice of science: observing, repeatedly, a small part of the environment with the
benefit of a body of past experience.

Along many parts of the Mid-Atlantic, South Atlantic, and Gulf of Mexico coasts, watermen
conduct these experiments daily, in waters near shore, where the effects of human activity on
estuarine health are particularly notable. Puttering in and out of the inlets and sounds, passing
behind barrier islands, fishers who sail—often from their homes—increasingly navigate a coastline that is changing in ways that threaten their ability to experience and to observe. Where
many watermen ply their trade, the material residues of what are fast becoming the dominant,
and dominating, paths of coastal development are often only too visible: high-rise condominiums,
speed boats and jet skis, marinas supporting yachting and sportfishing, and the false landscapes
of miniature and full-sized golf courses. As recently as the middle 1960s, many of the barrier
islands and coastlines of the Carolinas and Georgia were covered with brush and crossed by
sandy roads. With exceptions like Florida's Palm Beach or South Carolina's Hilton Head, their
topography had not changed appreciably since their formation two thousand years ago. Yet over
the past thirty years, coastal regions everywhere have been attracting more and more seasonal
residents, visitors, and settlers, making neighbors out of people with different histories and
with divergent, often conflicting views about what their futures should hold.

Historically, coastal peoples worldwide have witnessed the arrival and departure of strangers
of all kinds. In literature and film, seaports are often portrayed as surprising places, lovely and
lively yet often seedy and dangerous, and the protected inlets and bays of many seacoasts recall
great adventures of whaling, piracy, and refuge. Elizabeth Bishop's poem, "Arrival at Santos,"
captures the mixed feelings that ports generate:

> …The tender is coming,
> a strange and ancient craft, flying a strange and brilliant rag.
> So that's the flag. I never saw it before.
> I somehow never thought of there *being* a flag,
>
> but of course there was, all along. And coins, I presume,
> and paper money; they remain to be seen.
>
> .   .   .   .
>
> Ports are necessities, like postage stamps, or soap,
>
> but they seldom seem to care what impression they make,
> or, like this, only attempt, since it does not matter,
> the unassertive colors of soap, or postage stamps—
> wasting away like the former, slipping the way the latter
>
> do when we mail the letters we wrote on the boat,
> either because the glue here is very inferior
> or because of the heat. We leave Santos at once;
> we are driving to the interior (Bishop 103–104).

When Bishop wrote these lines in 1952, many seaports may not have cared much about what kinds of impressions they made. As working waterfronts, organized for commerce, fitted with rails and piers and lined with warehouses and workshops, they were landscaped essentially to receive, serve, and send off the maritime traffic of primarily commercial vessels and military fleets. Remnants of their importance to international relations and communication remain in structures as little-known as the relic dikes and canals of Georgia's rice plantations or as well-known as North Carolina's Fort Macon. Yet over the past thirty years many ports have begun to care, almost too deeply, about the impressions they make, leading to coastal landscapes that are more the result of passing disputes over aesthetics than they are the products of long, evolving trends in human communication and commerce.

Scholars studying Southern and Caribbean slave plantations that operated during the sixteenth and seventeenth centuries considered these massive enterprises total institutions: constructed social settings, like prisons or mental hospitals, that provided for enough daily human needs that most residents never had to leave their grounds. Total institutions are highly planned, highly designed, and nearly as scrupulously cared for as theme parks, yet unfortunately their development tends to be narrowly envisioned and inspired, drawing on the social and cultural backgrounds of only a handful of people. And no matter how much the planners attempt to control time, space, and rhythms of work and leisure, inevitably those who populate total institutions—whether prisoners, plantation slaves, or Disneyworld employees—bring their own cultural tastes and styles with them and, also inevitably, succeed in flavoring and undermining schedules, rules, and other aspects of the institutional regimen.

Many coastal landscapes today share with total institutions this narrowness of vision, resulting in miles of identical condominiums interrupted by similarly laid-out gated communities and disappointingly recycled names such as the Breakers, Cypress Landing, Bay Shore, or, my personal favorite, the Dunes. The phone book for the fastest growing coastal region in the United States—Wilmington, North Carolina—has over thirty listings that begin with the word "Ocean" and over ninety listings that begin with the word "Sea," including Ocean Crest and Sea Crest, Ocean Spray and Sea Spray, and Ocean Breeze and Sea Breeze. Whenever I arrive in an area that resembles Ft. Lauderdale, Florida; Myrtle Beach, South Carolina; Biloxi, Mississippi; or Ocean City, Maryland—all more or less interchangeable landscapes—I recall a passage in William Faulkner's *Light in August*. In that novel, a character named Byron Bunch muses about the name of another character (Lucas Burch) who goes by the pseudonym "Brown":

> There was no reason why his name should not have been Brown. It was that, looking at him, a man would know that at some time in his life he would reach some crisis in his own foolishness when he would change his name, and that he would think of Brown to change it to with a kind of gleeful exhalation, as though the name had never been invented (Faulkner 33).

While many parts of the coast have succumbed to over-development, resulting in a redundancy of names, other alternatives to the photocopied skylines of high rises and gated communities remain from the past and form incipient outlines for the future. Traditional uses of the coast include port and harbor development, commercial fishing, and seafood processing. Emergent alternatives include ecotourism and heritage tourism. Other alternative paths of development, less well-known or widely discussed, both recalling the past and portending the future, are the small social niches that develop in the wake of demographic changes we witness continually along the coast and the coastal plain. Hmong crafts fairs. Mexican grocery stores and cuisine. Mayan cooperatives and Mixtec methods of beautifying the land. All of these alternatives are as important to the continued health and well-being of the world's coasts as are gated communities, golf courses, theme parks, and mile after mile of condominiums, rental homes, and hotels.

Those who defend the overgrowth of conventional tourism, condominiums, and gated communities—most of which privatize lengths of coast—argue that these developments occur *beyond* the will of developers. That is, they assert that the driving force behind modern coastal landscapes is not the ambitions of a single group or class of individuals, but the irresistible power and the invisible hand of the free market. Yet reifying the market in this way—endowing it with nearly God-like influence—is suspect wherever an advanced and highly organized political apparatus exists. Along coasts throughout the Americas this is particularly so, because coast-lines, coastal plains, oceans, and sea lanes are deeply entangled in highly public debates over ocean and estuarine health, national sovereignty, commercial navigation, and common property. To invest free market forces with an immunity to very exact, detailed, and heavy human inter-vention in coastal environments and among coastal peoples is ludicrous and irresponsible.

Anthropologists have long argued that markets, like churches and laws, are deeply embed-ded in cultural processes, influenced not only by politics but also by beliefs about geography, history, demography, the arts, and myriad other processes. One implication of this is that the values attached to coastal properties and coastal lifestyles shift through time based on often highly unpredictable factors. During the eighteenth and nineteenth centuries, for example, the low country of the Carolinas, Georgia, and Florida was considered only marginally inhabitable, particularly during the summer months, when it was believed that "miasmas," or poisonous vapors believed to cause imbalances in the human body's fluids, seeped from the volatile inner core of earth (Wilms 1972). Coastal swamps were perceived to be particularly dangerous loca-tions, a factor that led to both the heavy use of slaves on coastal rice plantations and the establishment of inland communities that were used as summertime refuges.

With the benefit of germ theory, we may scoff at these beliefs today. Yet as recently as the mid-1990s, our own contemporary miasma—*Pfiesteria*—resulted in a precipitous decline in the value of North Carolina seafood and an exaggerated, irrational concern over the health of coastal living (Griffith 1999a, 1999b). As I write this essay in the spring of 2000, new evidence of encephalitis-carrying mosquitoes, perhaps arriving on ships and affecting coastal regions dis-proportionately, is stirring up similar concerns again. Coastal development that is geared toward conventional tourism and gated communities is particularly vulnerable to these health-oriented concerns and to other economic and environmental phenomena as well. All along southern coastlines, remnants of formerly popular tourist destinations, now deteriorating, collect prosti-tutes, drug dealers, petty thieves, and other criminals. But these places also attract law-abiding citizens like chambermaids and landscaping workers, who depend on many of the low-paying jobs that tourist areas create. More and more, throughout much of the South, many residents of those neighborhoods are new immigrants and refugees, recent arrivals with fleeting legal statuses and uneasy holds over housing and employment.

These areas reveal two related trends: (1) the popularity of tourist areas shifts through time, and (2) these shifts can transform swank resorts into dejected ruins. Still, such derelict paradises remain important to newer, often more exclusive tourist destinations as housing for tourism workers. For example, a neighborhood called Northwood in West Palm Beach began in 1923 as a development oriented toward seasonal residents, retirees, and tourists, with one-story stucco homes and small, charming motels with names like El Patio, Queen Anne, and Helen's. Today the motels of Northwood double as labor camps for workers who landscape golf courses and work in the plant nurseries and vegetable fields on the western edge of town, and many of the stucco houses have been either abandoned, converted into crack houses, or both. Ruined cars dot Northwood's streets, while piles of garbage laced with crack vials and syringes suffuse the subtropical air with perfumes of urine and decay. In the center of Northwood, a Baptist church has suffered from such a flight of its congregation that, to make ends meet and continue feeding lunches to the poor, it rents out a portion of its church on Sundays to Haitians for their Catholic services. The few businesses that survive in Northwood—beyond the pawnshops and liquor stores—are domestic violence shelters, AIDS clinics, and the offices of lawyers who take the cases of the desperate and dispossessed.

Even if new tourist destinations don't depend on former tourist destinations for housing, many neighborhoods that house tourism workers possess characteristics similar to Northwood, primarily because they are situated inside of or near major agricultural regions and house seasonal farmworkers under notoriously poor living conditions. The reason for this proximity is primarily climatic: the same weather conditions that attract tourists are also often ideal for the long or specialty growing seasons that agriculture requires. This isn't only true of the Central Valleys of California, which lie within minutes of many of the state's tourist regions. We find extensive apple orchards along the southern shores of Lake Erie, in the fingerlakes regions of upstate New York, in peach and apple growing regions all along the Blue Ridge Mountain chain, and in fresh vegetable production outside Ocean City, on Maryland's eastern shore.

We see quite clearly how this has played out over time in a place like Florida, where, only a few miles west and east of major tourist areas along both its coasts, we find neighborhoods and communities where farmworkers and tourism workers live side by side. Those familiar with the literature on farm labor along the eastern seaboard will readily recognize names like Immokalee, Indiantown, Homestead, and Belle Glade as well-known farmworker communities. In a book I published with several co-authors a few years ago, I described Immokalee as resembling:

> ...a densely populated inner-city ghetto far more than a small rural town. At the heart of one of the town's poorest areas is the supermarket parking lot where farm labor contractors meet their crews in the early morning. This gathering place of farmworkers is also known locally for its taverns and flophouses, for its drugs and prostitution, for its check-cashing services and drive-through liquor tunnels, and for muggings, bail bondsmen, and the restless idleness of the chronic unemployed (Griffith and Kissam et al., 33).

The potential for coastal development oriented toward the wealthy promotes a form of apartheid that compels us to consider alternative paths of coastal development with an eye toward preserving, through active intervention, social and cultural diversity. Although diversity—whether social, cultural, or biological—is intrinsically interesting, preserving cultural and social diversity is perhaps most important as a source of economic diversity and creativity: simply increasing development alternatives will help avoid the kind of overdependence on one source of revenue, income, jobs, and so forth that led to widespread despair throughout Pennsylvania and Ohio after the decline of steel mills. As coastal development alternatives compete for labor, territory, political favor, credit, and other social resources, it seems wise to consider the ways that each contributes to our appreciation of the coast. Such an exercise may facilitate our seeing them less as competitors for resources than as, in many ways, complementary.

Surely, for example, port and harbor development—devoted to big projects like dredging, channeling, inlet stabilization, and so forth—increases the opportunity for boating of all kinds, from large cargo and research vessels to smaller commercial and recreational crafts. Listening to those involved in port and harbor development, we learn that increasing access like this extends inland as well. A spokesperson for Wilmington Shipping, comparing Wilmington's port to Morehead City's, once said:

"Morehead is holding its own. That's a deep natural harbor pretty much. The draft problem is not there. Morehead is sort of stuck out, and only conducive for cargo going to probably the Raleigh area, because of the inland trucking...Morehead serves the northeast part of the state fine. Other than that, it's not conducive for Charlotte. For Charlotte, [a ship] would move over to Charleston before it would move over to Morehead City. The infrastructure in the state needs to be really addressed, like hooking up I-74 all the way to Charlotte, where it's not going through 35-mile-an-hour speed zones and stuff like that" (Interview 1998).

Coastal businesspeople who envision changes of this magnitude, considering the redesigning of not simply waterfronts but the landscapes of entire regions, may often lose sight of the smaller, intricate, and subtle interactions that occur among ecozones and populations of birds, fish, humans, raccoons, and others with whom we share our coasts.

Heritage tourism and ecotourism often possess the raw materials to draw people back from monumental schemes and grand histories, celebrating what is near at hand and dear to people who come to know and appreciate their immediate surroundings: what is, in a word, local. In 1994, the National Park Service asked me to speak with people on Maryland's lower Eastern Shore about plans for what they called a heritage corridor. This was to be a pathway extending from the Atlantic Ocean to the Chesapeake Bay, along which the park service would point out local history and design and erect interpretive signs to teach interested tourists about little-known features of the region's past. As with many projects like this, the idea for the corridor came from members of the chambers of commerce of small towns like Berlin, Snow Hill, Pocomoke City, and Crisfield. Its original designers thus represented but a small segment of local society, and the landmarks they wanted to highlight reflected primarily white, middle-class, small-town history. My job was to draw in the heritage resources from outlying farmers, from African Americans, and from watermen. I spent the summer of 1994 interviewing people, collecting obscure texts, and learning that all kinds of more and less hidden, more and less private celebrations of history and historical figures had occurred in southern Maryland for years.

My travels culminated in a visit to Smith Island in the Chesapeake Bay. The past twenty years have seen the total population of the island's three communities—Ewell, Tylerton, and Rhodes Point—decline nearly thirty-five percent, from approximately 450 to 300. Although a small number of new residents have relocated there, Smith Island has not yet experienced a large infusion of permanent outsiders, as have so many other maritime communities.

On Smith Island I met with Jennings Evans, a retired waterman who was lobbying the state for a visitors' center. He was something of a local historian, and we sat together on a bench outside Ruke's, the island's general store, until the greenhead flies chased us inside.

Seated at a table among the dry goods, Jennings anchored a gathering of locals, recalling for them the love and lore of the island. People joined and left our group, but conversation rarely strayed from the topics of Smith Island, watermen, or Chesapeake Bay history. A series of related incidents particularly enlivened the group. These were disputes over fishing territories that, between the early 1900s and 1947, caused the deaths of at least three watermen and were

(ABOVE) *Ruke's General Store and Seafood Restaurant. Known locally as "Ruke's," this is the most popular gathering place for locals and tourists in the Smith Island fishing village of Ewell. It is also the island's only year-round restaurant, famous for its crab cakes and Philly steak sandwiches.* (photo by Carmine Prioli)

(BELOW LEFT) *The Smith Island Center opened its doors to tourists on July 4, 1996. It grew out of community requests for a place where the island's history and culture could be preserved and shared with others.* (photo by Carmine Prioli)

(BELOW RIGHT) *Island historian and retired waterman Jennings Evans, discussing local history with visitors at the Smith Island Center.* (photo by Carmine Prioli)

responsible for simmering hostilities between communities, hostilities that, occasionally, boiled over into chaos at ball games or other public gatherings.

The disputes' origins were largely ecological. Centuries ago, Smith Island nearly connected with Tangiers Island, its neighbor to the south. But throughout recorded history the two islands have "migrated" through erosion, further and further from one another, widening Tangier Sound between them. As long as the land extended north from Tangiers and south from Smith to a point where it was easy to move by boat between the two islands, families were both more closely related to one another and more isolated from the mainland. According to watermen in Ruke's, Indians used to send young braves out to these islands as tests of endurance and lessons in how to hunt and fish. Picaroons—or casual pirates—roamed the waters around the islands and marshaled attacks on vessels throughout the Chesapeake and in Tangier Sound from a location on Smith Island, formerly called Rogues Point. Early settlers farmed, hunted, and fished to survive, farming for trade while hunting and fishing for subsistence.

Although families on the islands were closely related, political, economic, and ecological developments came between them along with the gradual growth of Tangier Sound. With the formation of the United States, politically the islands fell into different states' jurisdictions: Tangiers lay in Virginia territory and most of Smith, with the exception of its southern tip, became part of Maryland. State lines meant more during earlier centuries than they do today. Yet while part of Smith Island lay within Virginia territory, and while fishing was oriented more toward subsistence than commerce, the state line made little difference to the families of the islands. In the late nineteenth century, however, economic and ecological developments combined to increase the importance of state boundaries. The development of a market for oysters and, later, for crabs, increased the value placed on fishing for commerce instead of subsistence. At the same time, the loss of farmland from erosion and saltwater intrusion undermined the capacity of farming to sustain island commerce. With rising values placed on fishing and declining values on farming, Virginia and Maryland legislators moved to protect their fishing territories.

Because some of the finest oyster grounds lay in Virginia waters, and because crabs migrate north through the Chesapeake Bay, reaching the traps of Virginians first, Maryland crabbers—and hence most Smith Island crabbers—viewed their

Ewell's working waterfront. Looming over the traditional work-boats is the microwave tower that Tom Horton, author of An Island Out of Time: A Memoir of Smith Island in the Chesapeake, *found intrusive because its warning lights marred for him the island's "wilderness sanctity." Smith Islanders, however, harbor no such romantic notions of their locale and its isolated and often harsh lifestyle. They love their island, but they welcomed the tower "instinctively as a superior beacon" and for the way it provided better communication with the mainland (Horton, 15–16).* (photo by Carmine Prioli)

exclusion from Virginia fishing territories as illegitimate. By the end of the nineteenth century, Smith Island fishers routinely broke the law by taking oysters and crabs from Virginia waters, constantly anticipating the appearance of the Virginia marine police. A particularly good catch could be deadly. While most fishers, most of the time, fished with one eye trained on the horizon, a good catch might be so distracting that the police could cruise to a point close enough to engage the fishers in pursuit. In the early 1900s, the first fisher killed in the territorial dispute was John

Delivering a day's catch (4 bushels) of oysters. Smith Island, MD. (photo by Carmine Prioli)

Evans. Only fifteen years old, Evans was chased and shot in the head by a Virginia marine policeman. In 1910, another Evans, Thomas, exchanged gunfire with police on the water and was wounded. Weakened by the prolonged effects of the gunshot, he died a year later. On July 5, 1947, Earl Nelson, shot in the back while fleeing the police, died on Smith Island, in the shade of a tree near his dock.

In the search for heritage, the emphasis on stories like these illustrates the ambivalent feelings of fishing families toward the formal structures and regulations of the state. Just as cultural practices seep out of the edges of total institutions, the resistance of so many fishing families to regulations that further constrict their lifestyles constitutes an assertion of self*, community, and history against the smothering of wetlands with fairways and the barring of access to launching facilities through coastal gentrification. In disputes like these, fishers are not alone. Those who advocate the development of ecotourism are with fishers in their opposition to the kinds of growth that threaten wetlands, alter beaches, undermine waterways and endanger water-dependent plants and animals.

I find it ironic, though, that many of those who support ecotourism oppose, sometimes quite vehemently, commercial fishing as much as, or more than, they oppose development that routinely destroys wetlands, alters waterways, erodes beaches, and causes other major environmental problems. While it certainly is the case that some commercial fishing enterprises are organized to reap the greatest profits in the shortest time, regardless of environmental cost, no one who has spent much time with fishing families of the Mid-Atlantic, South Atlantic, Caribbean, or the Gulf of Mexico could conclude that this describes most commercial fishing operations. Instead, most fishers of these regions operate two or three twenty- to sixty-foot crafts, moving among different fisheries and based on shifting marketing opportunities and perceptions of fish

*In his essay, "Speech at the Beach: The Outer Banks Brogue," Walt Wolfram discusses the use of dialect by middle-aged watermen as an assertion of identity. See pp. 9–21, esp. p. 16, in this volume.

stocks that are, as I noted in the opening paragraphs, based on long-term interaction with marine resources. Targeting different species of fish and shellfish through the year involves using several different varieties of gear and becoming acquainted with the habits and habitats of the different species being sought. Fishing operations such as this thrive on diversity. Diversity of gear, vessels, fishing territories, and so forth prevents overspecialization and the kind of concentrated fishing effort we find in large, industrialized fishing fleets that target fish like menhaden, tuna, or groundfish and spawn huge onshore processing factories.

Current efforts to continue restricting the use of nets by commercial fishing families will lead to a reduction in diversity in two ways: (1) by reducing the number of commercial fishing families, many of whom depend heavily on nets during certain times of the year, and (2) by forcing more specialization among those types of gear that remain. Again, it is ironic that we find advocacy of this type among those involved in ecotourism, as expressed in the words of a hunting and fishing guide operating on North Carolina's Outer Banks. Speaking in opposition to net fishing, he said:

"I don't like it [netting fish] at all. Look, we learned a lesson a long time ago: you don't ride the train and kill all the buffalo in sight. And it ain't no different...I would have to assume that almost every species of fish is affected [by netting]...Inshore or offshore, I mean, I have a problem with it all" (Interview 1998).

The guide's analogy between netting fish and hunting buffalo is interesting, given that, in Florida, during public debates in the early 1990s over that state's eventual net ban, Florida fishers likened nets, not fish, to buffalo. They claimed that taking away nets from Florida fishers would have as negative an impact on them as hunting buffalo to near extinction sealed the fates of Plains Native Americans in the nineteenth century (Smith and Jepson 1993). One of the most poignant pleas for understanding came from the wife of a Florida fisherman who, following the net ban, moved to North Carolina to fish. She said:

"If I sound like a fatalist, perhaps I am because of the *really* bad experiences in Florida, just devastating experiences in Florida. Not for me personally, but for the people around me and for those families who not just depended on fishing: it isn't something you do to make a living; it's a way of life. I did not grow up in that, so stepping back from it, I see it's not getting up and going to work in the morning. It's *living* it, eating it, breathing it. And that might sound tremendously poetic, but it's true. The morning after the net ban, my husband woke up and I mean he was crushed; he didn't know what to do with himself. He had never ever in his whole life, since the time he could *walk*, not been able to get out on the boat and put a net overboard. He didn't know what to do. He said, 'I don't understand. My country asked me to go to Vietnam and I went to Vietnam.' He came back from Vietnam, he said, 'And my country said I can't make a living anymore. I have to find something else to do'" (Interview 1998).

Living it. Eating it. Breathing it. She is right that this might sound "tremendously poetic" and perhaps, to some, even trite, yet her point cannot be lost on anyone. For coasts to work, they need people who appreciate them this deeply, whose lives are so intertwined with coastal ecology that they occupy special crow's nests and widow's walks of observation. Families so situated move beyond the mere impressions of educated men. They compel us, once again, to recall Emerson's "Each and All," where the poet's eye is captured by "…delicate shells [that] lay on the shore." Fetching them home, he finds that his "sea-born treasures" have lost their beauty once removed from "…the sun, and the sand, and the wild uproar" (Emerson 9). Similarly, as maritime families disappear, we are all diminished. Accumulating local knowledge, interacting with the resource daily, they become uniquely qualified to assess the ways that opportunistic development and short-sighted growth are liable to remove Emerson's shell from its natural habitat or, worse, remove the habitat from around the shell.

Waterman James Barrie Gaskill and son Morton inspect crab pots. Ocracoke Island, NC. (photo by Ann Sabrell Ehringhaus)

REFERENCES

Quotations are from interviews with North Carolina coastal workers and residents and were conducted as part of a project for UNC Sea Grant College Program entitled, *Assessing Coastal Population Growth: Projected Needs and Management Issues* (1998–99).

Bishop, Elizabeth. *Elizabeth Bishop: The Complete Poems, 1927–1979*. NY: Farrar, Straus and Giroux, 1969.

Emerson, Ralph Waldo. "Each and All." In *Ralph Waldo Emerson: Collected Poems and Translations*. NY: The Library of America. Penguin Books USA, Inc., 1994.

Faulkner, William. *Light in August*. NY: Modern Library, 1939.

Griffith, David. *The Estuary's Gift: An Atlantic Coast Cultural Biography*. University Park, PA: Pennsylvania State Univ. Press, 1999. [1999a]

_____. "Exaggerating Environmental Health Risk: The Case of the Toxic Dinoflagellate *Pfiesteria*." *Human Organization* 58:2 (1999): 119–127. [1999b]

Griffith, David and Ed Kissam, Jeronimo Camposeco, Anna Garcia, Max Pfeffer, David Runsten, and Manuel Valdés Pizzini. *Working Poor: Farmworkers in the United States*. Philadelphia: Temple Univ. Press, 1995.

Horton, Tom. *An Island Out of Time: A Memoir of Smith Island in the Chesapeake*. NY: Vintage Press, 1996.

Jefferson, Thomas. *Notes on the State of Virginia*. In *The Portable Thomas Jefferson*, edited by Merrill Peterson. NY: Viking Press, 1975.

Smith, Suzanne and Michael Jepson. "Big Fish, Little Fish: Politics and Power in the Regulation of Florida's Marine Resources." *Social Problems* 40:1 (1993).

Warner, William W. *Beautiful Swimmers: Watermen, Crabs and the Chesapeake Bay*. Boston: Atlantic Monthly Press, 1976.

Wilms, Douglas. "The Development of Rice Culture in 18th Century Georgia." *Southeastern Geographer* 12:1 (1972): 45–57.

Acknowledgment: The author thanks the UNC Sea Grant Program for funding the project, *Assessing Coastal Population Growth: Projected Needs and Management Issues*. He also thanks his co-principal investigator, Jeff Johnson, for his work on the project.

Estuaries
Where the River Meets the Ocean

— Lundie Spence —

*I*f you walk the nearly 4,000 miles of North Carolina's salty shorelines, you'll find that only 350 miles face the ocean. The famous Outer Banks, Cape Hatteras, Emerald Isle, Wrightsville Beach, and quiet Sunset Beach are well-known tourist destinations, but ninety percent of the state's shoreline legacy lies behind our barrier islands. These shorelines edge estuarine waters—they reach far up along coastal rivers, then branch vein-like into tiny tidal marsh creeks. Because these estuarine waters and their fringing wetlands are held in public trust by the state of North Carolina, they belong to all citizens, not just to those who own adjacent property.

Unlike beachfront boundaries that are relatively stable, estuarine shorelines are not easily drawn or seen. The waters they border ebb and flow, flooding marshes, bathing grass meadows, lapping against trees in swamp forests. Walking these shorelines presents special challenges. Many are muddy entanglements of shrubs, cordgrass, tree stumps, and roots. Still, you can explore these vast natural treasures quite nicely—the way Native Americans and later inhabitants have done for hundreds of years—by boat, sail skiff, or canoe.*

The earliest people to explore the richness of the estuaries paddled dugouts to harvest fish and shellfish. In 1585 John White, the leader of Sir Walter Raleigh's ill-fated Roanoke Colony, painted watercolors illustrating people from the Late Woodland Algonkian culture catching fish with gear still used today. From a satellite perspective, the estuaries look very similar to the way they did during the pre-European contact period. However, a closer, more earth-bound perspective

*For maps of these estuaries and a discussion of their geological underpinnings, see Stanley R. Riggs's essay, "Life at the Edge of North Carolina's Coastal System: The Geologic Controls," in this volume, pp. 63–95, esp. pp. 81–92.

(ABOVE LEFT) *Native American fish-weir as illustrated by John White in 1585, later reproduced in this version by Theodore de Bry. The two men are poling their dugout canoe into the net to bail the fish trapped there as they swam with the current.* (courtesy of the North Carolina Collection, University of North Carolina Library at Chapel Hill)

(LEFT) *Contemporary commercial fishermen on Core Sound prepare to empty a pound net similar to the weirs used by the Algonkian natives for several hundred years. Note the wall of net in the background stretching toward the mainland shore.* (photo by Carmine Prioli)

(ABOVE) *Although much has changed since white settlers adapted Native American practices of harvesting the Carolina sounds, modern commercial fishermen still use circular dip nets to bail fish into their boats. Note the dip net resting on the transom of the canoe in the de Bry illustration* (ABOVE LEFT)*.* (photo by Carmine Prioli)

reveals that much has altered within the estuarine landscape in the past several hundred years. In fact, we know that estuaries are the *essence* of change.

Marine science has clearly shown—and simple observation tells us—that the sea level is rising. The increase is slow but steady, and has occurred over the long term: thousands of years. While experts debate the exact details, Stan Riggs, coastal geologist at East Carolina University, estimates the ocean rise to be about four inches per century. Old maps and charts of coastal North Carolina clearly show coastal plain lakes in Dare and Hyde counties that are now bays, such as Stumpy Point Bay and Wysocking

Bay. Conversely, Roanoke Island is shrinking, and some islands once located in the Albemarle Sound are now merely shoals. Since we are still in a warming trend from the last ice age (about 15,000 years ago), we can expect that the process of glacial melting will continue to flood river systems, broaden estuaries, and erode shorelines. Seasonal rainfall, too, affects the volume of waters in coastal rivers. Heavy rains in the late winter and early spring pump up river flows, sometimes gushing water over the banks and sweeping through the swamp forests. Scientists have shown that high water brings organic materials from the swamp floor down to the estuary, thus providing a natural source of nutrients.

Daily tides, waves, and currents continually stir water, mixing up a broth of nutrients for plants and animals. Occasionally, hurricanes and nor'easters bring enough rain to cause flooding far beyond the standard flood lines. These waters rapidly scour the shorelines, rearrange sediment, make inlets, wash upriver debris downstream, and affect estuarine water chemistry. In September 1999, Hurricane Floyd dumped more than twenty inches of rain in twenty-four hours on the coastal plain. This was preceded by Hurricane Dennis, which sat offshore causing sound and estuary waters to back up in the rivers. With this torrent of fresh water, rivers rose thirty to forty feet in many areas and produced the so-called five-hundred-year flood. Yet these events—disastrous to people, structures, and communities—are part of the natural dynamics of the estuary. Scientists predict that this pulse of floodwaters will affect the natural balance of the estuaries for years.

When people are responsible for changes to the water and adjacent land, these changes are called "anthropogenic" effects. Human influence now occurs at a faster rate than ever. Consider the impervious surfaces of highways, shopping centers, and building roofs that increase runoff, bulkheads, and revetments that increasingly divide the land from the water, and the practice of digging canals, ditches, and marinas.

Scientists use the word "estuary." Most folks call these bodies of waters "sounds" or "bays." In Texas, they are called "lagoons." Simply defined, an estuary is a place where fresh river waters meet salty ocean waters. Three factors shape North Carolina's estuaries: the low topography of the coastal plain; the flooding of coastal rivers due to rising sea level; and the presence of migrating barrier islands. North Carolina sounds are shallow basins, receiving river waters and having small outlets along the barrier islands for exchange with ocean waters. Thus, the estuaries hold most of the sediments and other substances coming downstream, as rivers dominate most of North Carolina's estuaries. Estuarine circulation can keep sediments, nutrients, and other substances stirring like soup inside the barriers for months to years. In fact, B.J. Copeland, an estuarine ecologist at North Carolina State University and articulate spokesperson for the marine environment, correctly refers to North Carolina's sounds as "sinks." And Copeland often laughs as he explains that many engineers require at least one semester of coursework to learn what our estuarine system tells us: that water runs *downhill*. The point is that upriver flow into the sounds is an important key to understanding the changing nature of the estuary and its ecological health. Whatever we do to the land and rivers in the Piedmont and coastal plain eventually is reflected in the waters of the receiving estuaries.

I. Estuarine Dynamics

North Carolina's estuarine system is a complex relationship of rivers, tidal creeks, marshes, swamps, and sounds encompassing at least 2.2 million acres. In the United States, it is second in size only to the Chesapeake Bay. While each of the major sounds has its own flavor of biology, chemistry, geology, history, and land use, all share basic estuarine dynamics.

First, the amount of sea salt in estuarine waters is less than that in the ocean because of dilution from the rivers. The closer you get to an inlet, the higher the salinity measurement. Average ocean water salinity is about thirty-two parts per thousand (thirty-two parts of salt to 1000 parts of water or, figuratively written, o/oo). You would not be surprised to measure salinity of 25 o/oo near an inlet and perhaps 5 o/oo or less in a mainland tidal creek. Low-salinity water is also called "brackish." Water of less than 5 o/oo salinity is fresh enough for the wild horses on barrier islands to drink. Currituck and Albemarle sounds are so far from inlets that you may not be able to measure salinity at all—the water is nearly fresh.

Second, there are two types of tides that affect the salinity and water level in estuaries. Lunar tides, which result from the gravitational pull of the moon and to some degree the sun, occur twice daily on the ocean beach and near inlets. Rising or incoming tides bring in ocean water with higher salinity and higher water levels to flood shorelines on a regular basis. Falling or outgoing tides allow river or creek fresh water to dominate, reducing the salinity and exposing shoreline flats to air and seasonal temperatures. Wind tides, which result from prevailing winds, push sound waters up creeks and rivers, again flooding the shorelines but on an irregular basis. Occasionally, winds will push waters out of the sounds and up against the barrier islands, perhaps breaking through the thin sandy islands, creating a temporary inlet.

Third, estuarine waters can have layers. The denser, saltier water creeps along the bottom, moving in and out with the lunar tides, while the lighter, fresher river water slips along the surface. This phenomenon is critical for larval crabs and shrimps, enabling them to migrate upriver to their estuarine nurseries. Their swimming power is so slight that they could never maneuver upstream in the surface waters. But when they sink near the bottom, the saltier waters, called a "salt wedge," carry them effortlessly to their destinations.

Dissolved oxygen, also known as DO, is necessary for any animal, fish, or shellfish to survive. Bottom layers can have less dissolved oxygen than layers closer to the surface, due to decomposition of organic material that settles downward. DO is measured in milligrams of oxygen per liter (mg/L), and ranges from 10 mg/L, which is high, to 0 mg/L, which is an anoxic condition. Measurements of DO less than 5mg/L can stress fish; lower DO can kill them. Waves and winds mix the layers, redistributing dissolved oxygen, plankton and nutrients.

Finally, estuarine systems and their fringing wetlands—swamps and marshes—have four distinct functions: (1) fish and shellfish, including commercially-caught species such as speckled trout, flounder, shrimp, and crabs, use sheltered parts of the system as a nursery, as it provides safe shelter and food rich sources; (2) the sounds are a storage basin or "sink" for nutrients, sediment, and all the other chemicals washed down by rivers and runoff flow; (3) swamps and marshes soak up excess runoff from the land and filter out some of the nutrients and sediments; (4) the barrier islands, estuarine waters, and fringing wetlands act as buffers to protect the mainland from storms and hurricanes. These functions point to the intrinsic value of estuaries.

II. Estuarine Diversity: The Topography and Waters Define the Biology

This brief review of the major estuarine systems in North Carolina reflects the diversity of these bodies of water. The northern sounds are more like wide basins, while the sounds south of Cape Lookout are often narrower and more closely associated with the ocean. Because the estuaries have different shapes, salinities, and river influence, the living resources also vary. A few of the more important species are presented to illustrate some patterns of lifecycles and the influence of humans on those cycles.

Currituck Sound

North Carolina's northernmost estuary is shallow Currituck Sound. Although it is about forty miles long and three to four miles wide, Currituck is less than ten feet deep. In the last five hundred years, at least five inlets have opened and closed connecting Currituck Sound to the ocean. Now they have all closed, drastically changing the ecology from a marine to a freshwater environment. Located about thirty miles north of Oregon Inlet—a source of ocean water—Currituck water is almost fresh with only 2 o/oo salt. You could drink it at the northern end. People there catch both freshwater fish, such as perch and bass, and blue crabs. A multi-year bloom of the exotic freshwater weed, Eurasian water milfoil (*Myriophyllum spicatum*), blanketed the sound during the 1970s and 1980s. While the thick growth of weed choked the water for motorboats and wind-driven piles of weed decayed with great odor on the shore, Currituck became a terrific habitat for large-mouth bass. However, occasional spikes of salinity in the 1990s have all but eliminated milfoil.

Currituck's water level is influenced mainly by wind tides. If a storm passes in just the right way with strong enough winds, the sound level can rise significantly. An example of this rise in water level occurred during the storm of March 1993. According to records of the U.S. Army Corps of Engineers, Currituck Sound rose six feet. It quickly fell again when the wind died or reversed direction.

Albemarle Sound

The Albemarle Sound is fed by the Chowan, Perquimans, Little, Pasquotank, and North rivers on the north side of the sound, and the Roanoke, Scuppernong, and Alligator rivers from the south side. Like Currituck, this sound has little salinity as rivers supply most of the water. Oregon Inlet flood tides only touch the Albemarle when driven by strong southeast winds.

Albemarle Sound stretches east-west for about fifty-five miles and averages seven miles wide and less than eighteen feet deep. Albemarle's almost five hundred miles of shoreline are fringed with cypress and gum swamp trees. This estuary receives sediments and nutrients from its river systems, and attracts striped bass, shad, and herring. These are anadromous fish. They live in the ocean, but spawn in fresh water, migrating up the rivers where the rich broth of algae and zooplankton provides food for larval and juvenile fish who mature and, in turn, swim to the sea.

The Albemarle-Roanoke River system supports the largest spawning population of striped bass, also known as rockfish, in North Carolina. Like other anadromous fish, they spend the majority of their life in the sea, but they migrate up the Roanoke River in the early spring. Stripers require flowing freshwater habitats in order to spawn successfully. Rain-swollen rivers suspend the eggs, bouncing them along the bottom, until they hatch, and then currents continue to transport larvae to nurseries in the lower, saltier estuary.

Because striped bass are so dependent on coastal rivers and estuaries for their spawning and nursery grounds, habitat destruction, river dams, sediment loads, plus heavy commercial and recreational harvests each contributed to depleted striper populations during the 1970s through the early 1990s. A moratorium on striper catches during the early 1990s resulted in a partial restoration of the population. Harvest for commercial and recreational fishers is now strictly regulated and managed.

Blueback or river herring have been another traditional anadromous spring fishery. Young herring depend on the estuary for their first growing season and migrate to the ocean to remain there until sexual maturity. The Albemarle Sound area has been the center of the commercial and recreational fisheries for river herring. Pickled and salted herring were sold in barrels from colonial days to the mid-1900s. However, the river herring population has declined drastically and most people once employed in the commercial industry have left or gone on to other occupations. Only enough fish remain for the seasonal restaurants along the Roanoke River to provide tourists and locals with short seasons for fried herring and rockfish stew (*Coastwatch*, Spring 2000).

**"Striper"—
Striped Bass,
Morone saxatilis** (sketch by Lundie Spence)

Roanoke and Croatan Sounds

The waters of the Currituck and Albemarle sounds connect to Pamlico Sound by passing around Roanoke Island through Croatan and Roanoke sounds, which are parallel to each other. Roanoke Sound is about eight miles long and one-half to two miles wide, averaging three feet deep. Croatan is about the same length, two to four miles wide and seven to ten feet deep. Because hurricanes can drive Oregon Inlet waters into the Albemarle using the reverse pathways, these sounds are important for drainage and circulation. They are also potential bottlenecks for anadromous fish and crabs. For example, it takes very strong southeast winds or hurricanes to bring blue crab larvae into the Albemarle.

Blue crabs are one of the most beloved of the estuarine species. Their story is told well in William Warner's *Beautiful Swimmers: Watermen, Crabs and the Chesapeake Bay* (1976) and in James

Blue Crab, **Callinectes sapidus** (sketch by Lundie Spence)

Michener's novel *Chesapeake* (1978). They are found throughout the sounds of North Carolina. Many a North Carolina child has caught feisty crabs off docks or from the shore, using chicken necks or fish heads as bait. Blue crabs are the most valuable commercial species in North Carolina, even surpassing shrimp in 1998. Hard crabs, which are caught in baited wire pots, sold live or steamed bright red, are a coastal vacationer's treat. Soft crabs, which have molted their hard shell in order to grow larger, have an increasing industry that ships live and frozen products to northern cities.

(ABOVE) *Father and son team Elzie and Adam Tosto, hauling crab pots in Pamlico Sound.* (photo by Carmine Prioli)

(BELOW) *Adam displaying a tray of soft crabs ready for shipment to northern markets. Once a fixture in coastal communities, family crabbing operations are—like other forms of commercial fishing—fast becoming a thing of the past.* (photo by Carmine Prioli)

In fact, most of the crabs harvested from North Carolina are shipped north, even though Tar Heels love picked crabmeat when they can get it. A study by Dave Eggleston at North Carolina State University estimates that the maximum sustainable yield (MSY) for blue crabs is between forty-eight and sixty million pounds per year. While average commercial landings between 1988–1998 were 49,251,586 pounds, worth $25,334,585, the 1998 commercial harvest exceeded the MSY with 62,068,133 pounds, worth nearly $45,000,000. Recently, however, the industry has seen a decline in mature female crabs, a sign of overharvest and/or poor environmental conditions. Management plans to protect the blue crab industry from its own success are underway (*Coastwatch*, High Season 1999).

Blue crabs use the whole estuarine system. Mature male crabs tend to hang out in more brackish waters. The mainland-side tidal creeks of the Pamlico and southern sounds and the Albemarle Sound are their preferred habitats. Mature female crabs are more frequently found in saltier waters. When the immature female approaches her terminal molt, which is when she can receive male sperm in order to produce eggs, she migrates into fresher waters.

The blue crab reproductive process is helped along by pheromones, chemical signals drifting in the currents cueing the males and females to find each other. Once mated, the female heads back toward the inlets, her abdomen flap extending with bright orange eggs. As the egg mass or "sponge" ripens, it turns dark—the black eyes of the young dominating the egg color. This female, called a "sook," releases the larvae directly into coastal waters. The larvae change shape many times before they finally molt into tiny, crab-like creatures that move through the inlet on the salty bottom layers or wind-driven surface currents.

Juvenile crabs then migrate from the sound sides of the islands across the bays to the thick salt marshes on the mainland sides, crawling along the bottom or swimming in the water column. Their nursery is in the marine grass meadows and tidal creeks. Their food is nutrient-rich detritus and small invertebrates found in the sediment. They also eat other blue crabs—it is certainly a survival of the fittest and fastest! The males stay near their nursery waters and females migrate eastward. While blue crabs can live five to eight years, their current maximum age is between two to three years—another sign of overharvest.

Pamlico Sound

The Pamlico Sound—with royal status among North Carolina's estuaries—covers over 2,000 square miles and represents fifty-six percent of the state's estuarine waters. It is about seventy miles long and ten to thirty miles wide. The Pamlico/Tar River and Neuse River drain an immense basin area and add sediment and nutrients from many coastal plain and Piedmont cities. The average water depth is sixteen feet, shallow enough for storms to stir up the bottom sediments. There is extensive shoaling around the shorelines and flood tide deltas at the inlets. The salinity varies with the tides and proximity to the Oregon, Hatteras, and Ocracoke Inlets, with ocean water of 32 o/oo and mainland creeks nearly fresh. Thus, you can find clams at the inlets and oysters along the inland shores.

The Pamlico Sound, including the Pamlico and Neuse River estuarine areas, constitutes the most important commercial fishery area in North Carolina. Spot, croaker, menhaden, shrimp, blue crabs, eel, weakfish, and flounder are among the twenty-plus species caught on a commercial basis.

Millions of oysters have been harvested from the southern extreme of Albemarle Sound to the South Carolina border. North Carolina was once famous for its salty shellfish, with Baltimore-based companies canning oysters in coastal towns. At the turn of the century, more than two million bushels were sold each year. By 1998, only about 45,000 bushels came in. In the past ten years, the most significant oyster-producing areas have been estuarine waters in Brunswick and New Hanover counties. Historically, Pamlico Sound had by far the highest production. Crab Slough, behind Oregon Inlet, still has the reputation for the tastiest, saltiest oysters. One clue to Crab Slough oysters is the presence of tiny, pink pea crabs inside the shell. As pea crabs prefer salty water, brackish oysters don't carry these tasty little morsels.

The demise of the oyster industry is mostly attributed to the destruction of the reefs. Storms with pounding waves can tear up an oyster reef, but harvesting methods, which dredge and tong up the reef habitat itself, have also been key culprits. Dermo, a parasite harmless to humans but fatal to oysters, invaded North Carolina sounds in the 1980s. Declining water quality reduced the survival of young oysters, delivering the final blow. With the loss of oyster-reef habitat, the homes of many other creatures have disappeared as well, including those of blue crabs, sea trout, drum, and striped bass (*Coastwatch*, Winter 2000). New management schemes and research in

restoration designs for oyster reefs have people hopeful that oysters can recover. A healthy oyster population will be a sign of the overall health of the estuaries.

Weakfish—also called gray trout or their Algonkian name, *squeteague*—are one of the most abundant fish in the Pamlico. Like other members of the drum family, they can produce drumming sounds by vibrating their air bladders. Recreational fishers target them. Commercial fishers use gill nets, pound nets, and haul seines to harvest them in huge numbers.

Weakfish spawn throughout the spring and summer in coastal waters. The larvae and juveniles are dependent on estuarine habitat as critical nursery areas. They seem to prefer the sandy/grassy shallows in bays and channels. During winter, the young of the year move into coastal waters near the shore. Following their first winter, the one-year-old fish move into the inlets and sounds to spawn for the first time. Their population numbers have fluctuated widely. A management plan is expected to rebuild their recently-depleted stocks. One focus is to develop gear that avoids harvesting juvenile weakfish as bycatch in other fisheries.

(ABOVE) *Weakfish,*
Cynoscion regalis

(ABOVE LEFT) *Eastern Oyster,*
Crassostrea virginica
(sketches by Lundie Spence)

The left-eyed summer flounder, the mainstay of many seafood restaurants, spend much of their early lives in the Pamlico. Spawning takes place in coastal waters. During the summer, larval fish enter inlets and settle on sandy bottoms in higher-salinity areas of estuaries. After their first year, summer flounder move into ocean waters to spawn and join coastal migratory groups.

Core and Bogue Sounds

The sounds south of the Pamlico are more confined because of the east-west facing barrier islands that hug the mainland. Core Sound and Bogue Sound are salty, narrow, shallow estuaries with lunar tides and an affinity for the coastal sea. Core is about thirty-six miles long where it joins with Bogue for another twenty-five miles. Each averages less than five feet in depth. Hard clams, along with blue crabs and shrimp, inhabit the sandy grass meadows and inlet shoals.

Southern Estuaries

The estuarine waters south of Bogue are intermeshed with salt marshes and small river systems. The nearby islands are almost attached to the mainland. Only tidal creeks and the Intracoastal Waterway (ICW) separate them. The sizable New River drains between Bogue and Stump Sound through the New River Inlet. Other basins are Topsail, Middle, Masonboro, and Myrtle. Bridges leap over the channels at Topsail, Wrightsville, Long Beach, and Ocean Isle.

Cape Fear Estuary

The Cape Fear River, pumping water drained from tributaries extending beyond Greensboro, bisects this southern island chain. Because no sandy island could exist in its flow, these estuarine waters are the only ones in North Carolina not contained in a sound. Brackish or low-salinity waters extend beyond Wilmington, with marshes and swamp forests defining the edges of the river.

In the early 1900s, schools of Atlantic and short-nosed sturgeon supported a healthy fishery, which exported caviar and high-quality seafood. These ancient-looking fish migrated up the Cape Fear to drop their eggs in the quiet, turbid waters. Sturgeons mature slowly and spend most of their early years in estuaries and large rivers. Their roe, or eggs, was one source of caviar. Overharvesting the reproductive stock created an inevitable decline. The population decrease is also attributed to habitat destruction, the construction of dams and locks, and general loss of water quality. The spawning schools have all but stopped, and the short-nosed sturgeon is now listed as an endangered species.

III. Ecological Patterns

Because North Carolina's estuaries are situated on the ecological divide between temperate and subtropical systems, they support a rich diversity and number of species. Thus, some plants and animals are at their northern limit (e.g., palmetto palms and red snapper), while others are at their southern limit (e.g., bayberry shrubs and black drum).

Researchers have identified the importance of North Carolina sounds to other Mid-Atlantic fisheries. Several commercial fish species spawn just outside of Oregon Inlet and the larval fish enter the Pamlico Sound nursery areas. Later, they form schools migrating up to the Chesapeake Bay and more northern coastal waters. This illustrates one of the functions of the estuary: a nursery. Eight major users—spot, croaker, menhaden, shrimp, blue crabs, herring, weakfish, and flounder—represent important seafood and industrial species.

Estuarine food webs are complex and contain many short food chains. Phytoplankton, blooming sometimes out of control, supports the grazers and is the basic level of production in the estuary. It is supplemented by detritus-based food chains. Phytoplankton—diatoms, dinoflagellates, and other tiny, single-celled algae—reach peak abundance in the winter and early spring. Some blooms may also occur during the summer. Young menhaden swim in giant schools in the Pamlico. Their mouths are wide open, scooping plankton onto their gill rakers. Clams in the sand flats extrude flexible tubes to siphon gallons of water, removing the plankton as food.

Decaying marsh grasses covered with nutritious bacteria form detritus-based food chains. The broken stems of salt marsh cordgrass (*Spartina alterniflora*) and needlerush (*Juncus roemerianus*) are carried out of the marshes by tides, broken into bits by waves, and slowly consumed by bacteria. These particles drift in the water column, at times settling to the bottom only to have waves bring them back into circulation. Polychaete worms waving feathery antennae dot the estuarine bottoms, competing with crabs and oysters for the detritus-laden water, which they filter with gills. Schools of croaker, gray trout, speckled trout, spot, and mullet feed on the worms, crabs, and other invertebrates.

Seagrass Meadows

The underwater meadows of seagrasses fringe shallow, sandy bottoms of the estuary. Seagrasses are real plants with roots, stems, and blades. Some even have flowers set in gelatinous sheaths. Earlier in this century, there were extensive grass beds where the sounds were shallow enough for light to be transmitted to the bottom. On the mainland side, the beds have shrunk to small patches or are totally lost. Poor water quality that includes excess nutrients and sediments has degraded the habitat. Remaining grass beds include tapeweed (*Valisneria americana*) and wigeon-grass (*Ruppia marina),* which grow in brackish estuarine systems, while eelgrass (*Zostera marina*) has more extensive beds on the back sides of barrier islands, specifically in Bogue and Pamlico sounds. Seagrass meadows are habitats for juveniles and adults of many species—clams, scallops, flounders, stingrays, shrimp, and crabs.

One method of harvesting hard clams (*Mercenaria mercenaria*) in the Pamlico/Bogue bottoms is called clam-kicking. A propeller wash can literally dig out a swash in the sediment, throwing clams back into a collecting basket. If you fly over the sounds, the clam-kicking trails are clearly visible in the seagrass meadows below. This method of harvesting is a subject of debate between those who are concerned about habitat protection and others whose living depends upon seafood harvesting.*

Estuarine Wetlands

Salt marsh cordgrasses, rushes, and sedges form fringing or island marshes in the estuaries. These wetland plants live between water and land ecosystems, forming a critical interface with some of the highest productivity—capturing of carbon—on this planet. The biomass production can be as high as five to ten tons of organic matter produced per acre per year. Compare that to a typical wheat field producing one ton per acre per year or the open ocean, where production is less than one-half ton per year. The saturated marsh soils are fertilized by river-borne nutrients on each regular or irregular tide. Each spring, a new crop grows. Each winter, old plant material, detritus, is redistributed by the tides.

Salt marshes contain few plant species and are typically a monoculture. Salt marsh cordgrass (*Spartina*) tolerates high-salinity water; black needlerush (*Juncus*) is more common in brackish, irregularly-flooded wetlands. There are ten plant species which are legal indicators of salt marsh habitats. Most tolerate regular, partial submersion, which allows them to collect suspended sediment and anchor it in their root system, thus building up the shoreline. Though flexible, blades of grass are able to absorb wave energy from the strongest storms, buffering the shore from acute erosion. The roots and blades filter and hold land and rainwater runoff, sequestering more sediments and excess nutrients. In the last fifty years, wetlands, particularly in Carteret, Dare, and Hyde counties, were ditched, disrupting the natural drainage patterns. Instead of reducing the mosquito population—the objective of the engineering effort—this project created stagnant pools, which were not only perfect for mosquito growth, but were also cut off from natural predators present in tidal creeks. Aerial flights over these wetlands still show the fifty-year-old furrows.

---

*For more on the issue of habitat protection vs. commercial fishing interests, see David Griffith's essay, "Coasts in the Works: Impressions of Working Waterfronts," in this volume, pp. 37–48, esp. pp. 44–46.

Great Blue Heron, Ardea berodias (sketch by Lundie Spence)

Estuarine wetlands are habitat for many resident and transient birds. They are the winter feeding grounds for migrating waterfowl such as geese, swans, and ducks. The secretive Clapper Rail cries loudly and builds nests in the *Spartina* marsh grass perched over high tides. Stately heron and egrets wait patiently in tidal creeks to stab minnows and crabs. Ibis swish their long bills through the mud, locating small invertebrates. Red-winged blackbirds perch on the long grasses, quick to capture insects. Sparrows and warblers move through the shrub thickets with quick bursts of flight.

The beauty of the marshes and the presence of wetland birds are drawing more visitors to coastal back roads. The late Dirk Frankenberg, who was an estuarine scientist at the University of North Carolina at Chapel Hill, suggested driving routes for the eco-tourist in his guides to the North Carolina coast.

Threats to the Ecological Health of Estuaries

Estuaries are not immune to natural disasters. In November 1987, a bloom of "Red Tide" toxic dinoflagellates swept into Bogue Sound, just south of Cape Lookout. The toxins released by the organisms upon their death affected the nervous and respiratory systems of aquatic creatures. Fish or crabs that could swim or crawl away did, but shellfish either closed up or were suffocated. While many oysters survived, thousands of bay scallops, residents of the seagrass meadows, were more vulnerable and died. Not only were the adults killed, so were the young of the year clinging to the grass blades. Recovery of the bay scallop took several years. Even humans reported both respiratory problems from the airborne toxins and numbness after eating shellfish.

Most threats to the health of estuaries are anthropogenic, that is, man-made. A 1996 study by Barbara Doll and Andrew Colburn identified fifteen land-use and human activities that have the potential to degrade estuarine waters. These included municipal wastewater treatment plants, pulp and paper waste, aquaculture, boat and barge traffic, fishing practices, marinas, seafood processing, land-disturbing activities, agriculture, on-site waste treatment/septic systems, golf courses, residential and commercial development, industrial sites, hydromodifications such as dredging and stream channelization, and wetland alteration.

The effects of anthropogenic input on the changing health of the estuarine system are often subtle and difficult to correlate. Multiple impacts and cumulative impacts pose scenarios that are difficult to identify. It's important for us to realize that little of the damage to the estuarine environment has a single source or a single effect. Scientists and managers continue to debate and request additional studies as they detect symptoms of degrading estuaries. These signs are evident in declining fisheries, poor water quality, harmful blooms of toxic dinoflagellates such as *Pfiesteria piscida* and cyanobacteria (blue-green algae), and shrinking habitats of wetlands, oyster reefs, and seagrass meadows.

Protecting the Estuaries

North Carolina is nationally known for its progressive coastal protection policies. The Coastal Area Management Act (CAMA) of 1974 contains policies that protect the estuaries as areas of environmental concern (AECs). Permits from the North Carolina Division of Coastal Management (NCDCM) are required for any building or physical alteration that affects shorelines, wetlands, and bottomlands. In addition, the North Carolina Division of Water Quality has policies that more specifically protect water quality (e.g., the river basin management plans). The North Carolina Division of Marine Fisheries, which manages fish and shellfish stocks, has worked with other state agencies to focus on the health of estuarine habitats.

Some estuarine areas have been identified and placed under special oversight. In 1982, the North Carolina National Estuarine Research Reserve (NCNERR) was established to preserve these certain estuarine habitats for long-term research, monitoring, education, and other compatible uses. The NCNERR consists of four separate components: Currituck Banks, the Rachel Carson Reserve, Masonboro Island, and Zeke's Island. NCDCM manages these resources as part of a national system of estuarine reserves. The U.S. Department of the Interior manages a number of wildlife refuges, and the Cape Hatteras and Cape Lookout National Seashores provide more federal management and protection. In addition, some of North Carolina's state parks—Goose Creek State Park, Hammock's Beach State Park, and Carolina Beach State Park—border estuaries.

Conclusion

Understanding estuarine relationships requires these key words: complex, changing, connections, and productive. North Carolina's estuarine system is complex and changing. Connections exist between land and sea, marsh and estuary, state and federal agencies, science and policy, and coastal and inland people. Connections exist geographically between North Carolina's sounds and adjacent coastal waters, and also Virginia's and Maryland's Chesapeake Bay and South Carolina's coastline. Our estuaries are highly productive, integrated systems.

The early people of coastal North Carolina left artifacts showing their dependence on estuaries—dugouts, shell middens, and post hole remains of lodges indicating the presence of small coastal communities. Their imprint on the land and waters was minimal, but then their population density was low. In this new millennium, our twenty-first century impact is much more intrusive, and the already-large coastal population is increasing.

Estuaries have tremendous economic value. Coastal North Carolina's economic base is changing from traditional commercial fisheries to tourism and recreation. While the state has strong policies toward protection and management, increasing population and development continue to add stresses upon the natural system. Regulations are only part of the effort. Private citizens, advocacy organizations, "river keepers," and school groups are the watchdogs of our environment. Public support will ultimately preserve what we have and restore what has been lost.

RECOMMENDATIONS FOR FURTHER READING

Coastwatch, the magazine published by NC Sea Grant, has several articles on estuaries. You can order the following from the NC Sea Grant office (Box 8605, NCSU, Raleigh, NC 27695-8605):

"Blue Crab: Study Reveals New Secrets" (High Season 1999).

"Budding Scientists: Teens Join Cutting-Edge Research" (Holiday 1999).

"Currituck Sound: In A Pickle" (November/December 1994).

"Herring" (Spring 2000).

"Old Currituck" (Spring 1999).

"Oysters" (Winter 2000).

"Recipe for an Estuary" (May/June 1994).

"The Big Ditch" (Winter 1999).

Doll, Barbara and Andrew Coburn. *Protecting Coastal Resources from Cumulative Impacts: An Evaluation of the North Carolina Coastal Area Management Action.* Raleigh, NC: NC Sea Grant Publication (1996): UNC-SG-96-12.

Doll, Barbara and Lundie Spence. *Coastal Water Quality Handbook.* Raleigh, NC: NC Sea Grant Publication (1999): UNC-SG-97-04.

Frankenberg, Dirk. *The Nature of North Carolina's Southern Coast: Barrier Islands, Coastal Waters, and Wetlands.* Chapel Hill/London: UNC Press, 1997.

_____. *The Nature of the Outer Banks: Environmental Processes, Field Sites, and Development Issues, Corolla to Ocracoke.* Chapel Hill/London: UNC Press, 1995.

Griffith, David. *The Estuary's Gift: An Atlantic Coast Cultural Biography.* University Park, PA: Pennsylvania State Univ. Press, 1999.

Lippson, Alice J. and Robert L. Lippson. *Life in the Chesapeake Bay.* Baltimore, MD: Johns Hopkins Univ. Press, 1997.

Michener, James. *Chesapeake.* NY: Random House, 1978.

Pilkey, Orrin H., William J. Neal, Stan R. Riggs, et al. *The North Carolina Shore and its Barrier Islands: Restless Ribbons of Sand.* Durham, NC: Duke Univ. Press, 1998.

Spence, Lundie. *Coastal Geology.* Raleigh, NC: NC Sea Grant Publication (1989): UNC-SG-78-14-A.

Warner, William W. *Beautiful Swimmers: Watermen, Crabs and the Chesapeake Bay.* Boston: Atlantic Monthly Press, 1976.

Life at the Edge of North Carolina's Coastal System
The Geologic Controls

— Stanley R. Riggs —

The shore is an ancient world, for as long as there has been an earth and sea there has been this place of the meeting of land and water. Yet it is a world that keeps alive the sense of continuing creation and of the relentless drive of life. Each time that I enter it, I gain some new awareness of its beauty and its deeper meanings, sensing that intricate fabric of each with its surroundings.

—Rachel Carson, *The Edge of the Sea* (1959)

Introduction

The human history of "life at the edge of the sea" in North Carolina is unlike that of other land-based cultures due to the high-energy and extremely dynamic character of the coastal system. Native Americans inhabited coastal North Carolina for over 10,000 years; however, little archeological record of their occupancy has been preserved.* Even the archeological record of the first European settlement on Roanoke Island in 1587, often referred to as the "Lost Colony," has been all but obliterated by the dynamic processes and rapid rates of change taking place within our coastal system. The high-energy processes resulting in continuous evolutionary change will also prevent any great monuments from our modern coastal civilization from surviving into antiquity.

Today, the processes of change continue to take their toll as every nor'easter and hurricane place their mark upon the shifting sands of time. Change is the only constant within the coastal

---

*For more on pre-colonial native American culture, see Randy Daniel's essay, "Archaeology and Ancient Cultures at the Edge of the Sea," in this volume, pp. 97–111.

system and this change happens at rates that defy conventional human perception and development patterns on more stable and inland terrains. This is our heritage for "life at the edge of the sea."

Physical Setting of the North Carolina Coastal System

A map of North Carolina's drainage basins (Fig. 1) demonstrates dramatic geographic differences in the character of the coastal system. A vast and complex network of creeks, streams, and rivers moves the surface water systematically off the uplands of the Blue Ridge, Piedmont, and

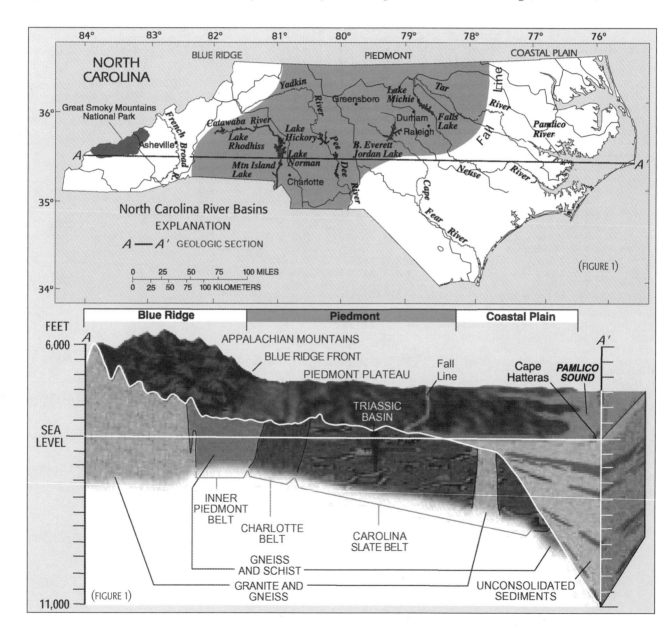

(FIGURE 1)

coastal plain provinces toward the Atlantic Ocean. These never-ending ribbons of fresh water flow through their self-eroded valleys downhill to sea level, where they intermingle with the salty waters of the Atlantic Ocean. At sea level there is a broad, low-sloping transition zone that

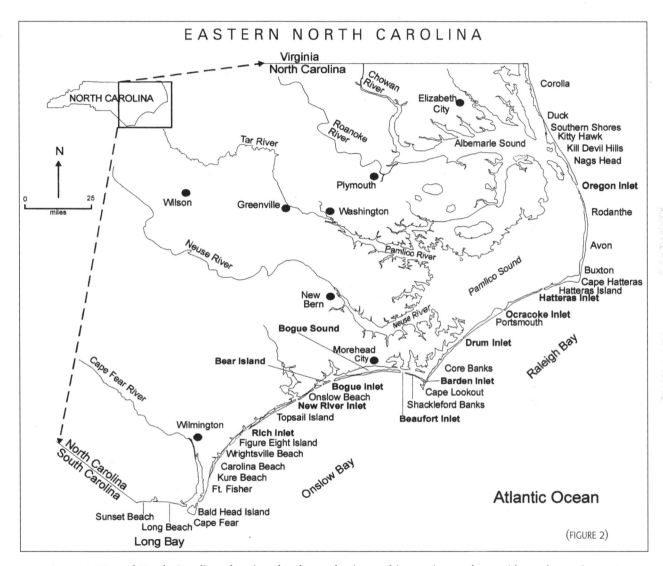

(FIGURE 1) *Map of North Carolina showing the three physiographic provinces along with a schematic west to east cross-section (A–A') showing the underlying geologic framework. Notice that (1) the coastal plain is composed of a seaward-thickening wedge of younger marine sediments deposited on top of the older crystalline rocks of the Piedmont, and (2) the major trunk rivers flowing across the coastal plain have their origins in and drain the Piedmont province.* (figure from the U.S. Geological Survey)

(FIGURE 2) *Location map of the North Carolina coastal system showing the vast estuarine zone, or mixing basins, that occur between the fresh-water riverine and salt-water oceanic systems. Separating the estuarine and oceanic zones is the barrier island sand dam with a few small inlets/outlets through the dam allowing the ultimate escape of fresh water into the Atlantic Ocean.*

forms the vast estuarine system connecting the rivers to the ocean (Fig. 2). The estuaries are great mixing basins of fresh and salt waters within the coastal system.

Fronting this estuarine zone is a narrow strip of sand that acts as a dam between the estuaries and ocean (Fig. 2). The interaction between high-energy storms on the ocean and the low-sloping land of the coastal plain produced this extensive strip of barrier islands. The sand dam is broken by a series of small openings commonly called "inlets" that are essential for ultimately discharging the riverine fresh water into the sea. The sand barriers are like icebergs— only a small portion rises above the sea surface, and the greatest portion is hidden below sea level. The barrier island is perched on a long sloping ramp that extends seaward onto the inner continental shelf from twenty-five to seventy feet below. This ramp and associated barrier islands function solely as energy-absorbing buffers between the waves, tides, and currents occurring within the ocean and the adjacent landmass.

The general geologic map of the North Carolina coastal plain (Fig. 3) suggests major differences between the northern and southern coastal regions that reflect the difference in their geological heritage. A line drawn from Raleigh through Kinston and Cape Lookout separates the coastal system into the northern and southern coastal provinces. Each province is underlain by a unique geologic framework that results in the formation of distinctive types of rivers, estuaries, and associated barrier islands and inlets.

The unique geometry of the North Carolina barrier islands formed by the capes and their associated sand shoals further characterizes the coastal system. The coast consists of four cuspate-shaped compartments (Fig. 3), each with its own characteristic physical and chemical dynamics and resulting biological and geological components. These compartments are known as "cuspate embayments" because of their cusp-like shape and are defined by the capes and cross-shelf cape shoal structures. Each cape contains a shore-perpendicular sand shoal that extends seaward for ten miles (Diamond Shoals off Cape Hatteras), fifteen miles (Lookout Shoals off Cape Lookout), and thirty miles (Frying Pan Shoals off Cape Fear). These vast shallow-water shoals give the North Carolina coast the dubious honor of being the "graveyard of the Atlantic."

In the northern province, Hatteras compartment faces northeast to east and reaps the head-on impact of frequent nor'east storms. By contrast, Raleigh Bay compartment is generally southeast-facing and only receives glancing blows from powerful nor'easters. In the southern province, Onslow Bay and Long Bay compartments face from southeast to south and are dominated by broad, shallow, and rock-floored continental shelves. This setting results in nondestructive offshore winds and waves from nor'east storms and a greater proportion of direct hits from less frequent, but very destructive tropical storms and hurricanes.

To better understand our coastal system, we must also understand the basic geologic controls that define the two coastal provinces. It is the spatial geometry in consort with the geologic framework that defines the character of the North Carolina coastal system: size and type of estuarine and barrier island habitats, water salinity, wave and tidal energies and processes, plant and animal communities, and problems resulting from human interaction and intervention.

Geologic Framework of the North Carolina Coastal System

Relatively old rocks (Fig. 3) underlie the coastal system in the southern province, from Cape Lookout south to the South Carolina border. These rocks range in age from the Upper Cretaceous (about 90 million years ago) through the Pliocene (about 1.6 million years ago). In this region, only a thin, highly variable skin of surficial sand and mud of Quaternary age has been deposited during the last 1.6 million years. These older units are generally composed of hard rocks, including mudstone, sandstone, and limestone. They are associated with a large geologic structure called the Carolina Platform that underlies the region between Myrtle Beach, South Carolina, and Cape Fear, North Carolina. This structural platform rises close to the earth's surface, causing the

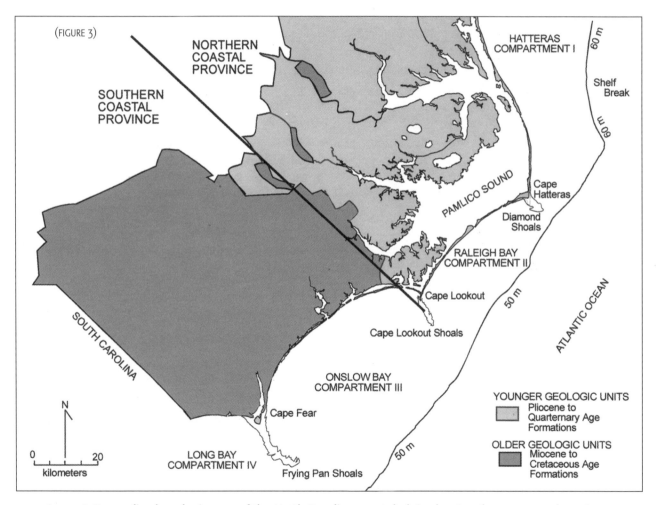

(FIGURE 3) *Generalized geologic map of the North Carolina coastal plain showing the two coastal provinces and the four geomorphic compartments of the North Carolina coastal system. These cuspate embayments are defined by the classic Carolina capes and their associated cross-shelf sand shoals. Due to different spatial geometry, the coastal system within each compartment is significantly different from the other compartments.*

older and harder rocks to be eroded and truncated by the shoreline (Fig. 3). Consequently, this erosional topography has relatively steep slopes with common exposures of the older rock units that control the shoreline geometry along the southern coastal system.

In contrast, the coastal system in the northern province, from Cape Lookout north to the Virginia border, is underlain primarily by younger sediments of Quaternary age (Fig. 3). These sediments generally consist of slightly consolidated to unconsolidated mud, muddy sand, sand, and peat that thicken northward to fill the subsiding Albemarle Embayment with up to 250 feet of sediments. The generally-soft sediments were deposited during the many sea-level fluctuations that resulted from multiple glaciations and deglaciations of the Quaternary ice ages during the past 1.6 million years. Consequently, a gentle depositional topography is common along the present northern coastal system, and the older rock units are deeply buried beneath these surficial sediments.

These two different geologic frameworks produce dissimilar sediment supplies and land slopes between the southern and northern provinces. The southern province is characterized by an average slope of three feet per mile, compared to 0.2 feet per mile in the northern province. Thus, rising sea level floods the disparate slopes, producing different kinds of barrier island-inlet systems and associated estuaries (Fig. 3). The steeper slopes of the southern province produce eighteen short, stubby barrier islands with eighteen inlets and narrow back-barrier estuaries. The gentle slopes of the northern province produce long barrier islands with only four inlets, and an extensive sequence of drowned-river estuaries in the vast Albemarle-Pamlico estuarine system. These northern barrier islands project seaward, forming the famous Cape Hatteras and associated Outer Banks—a sand dam that semi-isolates the Albemarle-Pamlico estuarine system from the ocean.

The Barrier Island Sand Dam

Barrier Islands and Storms

The line where the ocean meets the land, the shoreline, is a zone of extremely high energy. This energy occurs in the form of waves, currents, astronomical tides, and storm tides and is derived from two important sources. First is solar energy that differentially heats the earth's atmosphere, ocean, and land surfaces and drives the great heat pump operating between the air-sea-land interfaces. Second is the gravitational force occurring between the moon, sun, and earth as they revolve about each other in their endless journey through space. These great and continuous inputs of energy must either be converted to some other form of energy or released back into space. Otherwise, the planet would quickly become uninhabitable. The energy that stays within our earth system must do work. Energy can also change form, but it cannot just disappear.

Some of the energy input into the oceanic system does the geologic work of building and maintaining barrier islands and beaches. These high-energy, dynamic coastal systems are event-driven by individual storms or sets of storms, resulting in massive changes within time frames of hours to months. The cumulative impact of multiple storms and numerous winter storm seasons severely erodes the front side of barrier islands, builds up the back side of the islands, and modifies inlet/outlet systems, closing some while opening others, moving them about like chess pieces on a geological game board.

Barrier Islands and Their Inlet/Outlet Systems

Associated with barrier islands are small holes through the sand dam called inlets. These inlets played a critical role in the history of North Carolina by allowing development of inland ports for ocean-going shipment of goods and movement of people (Fig. 2). But "inlets" really should be called "outlets"! This is because their main function is to let the fresh water flowing off the land pass through the barrier island sand dam and discharge into the ocean, which is the ultimate depository for water on earth. However, once an outlet is open, then it also functions as an inlet. Astronomical tides create water level differentials along the coast, forcing a tidal exchange of water through the inlet and between the ocean and adjacent estuaries. Thus, astronomical tides alternately pump water in and out of inlets based upon the regular rhythms of the lunar and solar orbital motions. This tidal pumping produces strong tidal currents that maintain outlet-inlet systems on the short-term scale of hours to years. Storms and the associated storm surges also produce differences in coastal water levels that lead to extreme tidal currents through inlets, but on a basis that is dependent upon the irregularity of climatic patterns. These irregular storm tides often result in much higher water levels, with stronger currents that maintain outlet-inlet systems on the longer-term scale of days to centuries.

On high-energy barrier islands and within dynamic outlet-inlet systems, geologic time is synonymous with human time. Geologists are generally perceived as dealing only with millions of years of geologic time. Yes, when we are considering earth history we do think in terms of millions and billions of years. However, when we consider modern earth processes such as earthquakes, volcanic eruptions, riverine floods, and barrier island dynamics, we are concerned with time scales of seconds to centuries. These are geologic events that occur in time frameworks associated with human society. They range from individual life spans to multiple generations and often are tied directly to the rise and fall of specific civilizations. At this scale, *geologic time is human time*!

Role of Paleotopography and Sand Supply in Barrier Island Dynamics

Barrier islands are more than just piles of sand. Today, the North Carolina coastal plain has a specific morphology or topography that is a product of the depositional and erosional processes of the past 20,000 years. However, during the time period between 20,000 to 10,000 years ago, large portions of the earth's land surfaces were buried beneath miles of glacial ice. The water to build these glacial masses came from the world's oceans, causing sea level to drop. This placed North Carolina's ocean shoreline about 420 feet below present sea level and between twenty to sixty miles seaward of the present shoreline. Thus, the coastal plain, with its upland and associated river valley topography, extended completely across the present continental shelf.

During the time period between 10,000 years ago and the present, the earth's climate has warmed, causing glacial ice to begin melting and global sea level to begin rising. The former cold, semi-arid, boreal climate of North Carolina began its slow shift toward the present humid temperate climate of today. The initial coastal zone formed during the low sea-level stand where the ocean surface intersected the land surface. During the subsequent deglaciation, the barrier

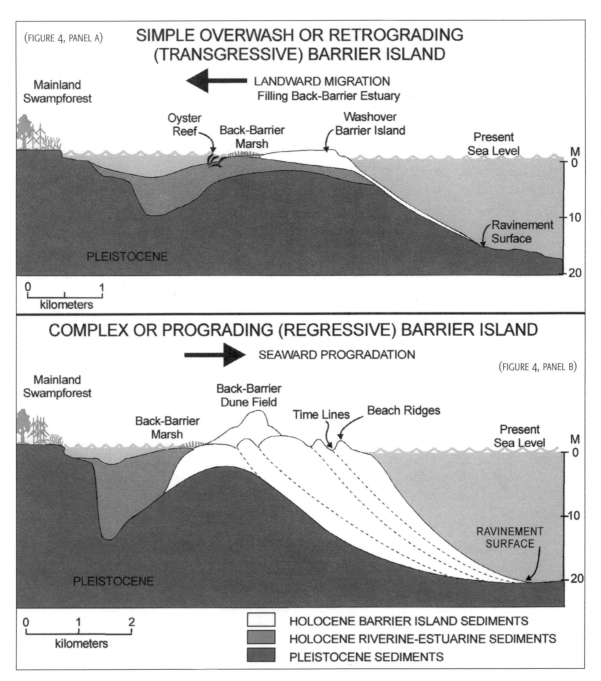

(FIGURE 4) *Schematic cross-sections showing the geologic framework of two different types of barrier islands.* (PANEL A) *Formation of a simple overwash barrier island in response to conditions of severe sediment starvation. Notice how thin and narrow the barrier island sand pile is and how it is perched on top of the shallow estuarine mud and peat sediment that frequently crop out in the beach and shoreface.* (PANEL B) *Formation of a complex barrier island in response to the periodic input of new sediment within a sediment-rich coastal segment. Notice how thick and wide the barrier island sand pile is and how it totally buries the estuarine mud and peat occurring behind the barrier island.*

islands and estuaries have migrated upward and landward across the continental shelf and buried the old land surface. This now-buried paleotopography and the underlying geologic sediments maintain very strong controls over the modern coastal system that has produced a new or modern

(FIGURE 5) *Role of sediment supply to the formation of simple overwash and complex barrier islands.* (PANEL A) *A 1996 close-up photo of the marsh mud and peat cropping out on the beach of the sediment-starved overwash barrier island. This photo was taken immediately after a storm at Onslow Beach, when the sand had been temporarily eroded away.* (PANEL B) *A 1969 close-up photo of the algal-covered, rocky beach at Fort Fisher. This rock outcrop consists of Pleistocene cemented sandstone that underlies the beach and acts as a rocky headland, controlling the patterns of shoreline erosion.* (PANEL C) *An oblique 1984 aerial photo, looking northeast across Roanoke Sound in the foreground, Nags Head Woods maritime forest on the right side, Kill Devil Hills in the background, and the Atlantic Ocean at the top of the photo. Nags Head Woods is being overrun by the very large and active Run Hill dune field. On the upper left portion of the photo is the stabilized Kill Devil Hill and Wright Brothers monument. When the Wright Brothers used this area to test-fly their planes, the upper portion of the barrier now occupied by the town was a vast unforested and active dune field (see Figures 6–9 and 10A and B).* (PANEL D) *Close-up photo of the northwest side of Run Hill as it migrates over the Nags Head Woods maritime forest and estuarine salt marshes of Roanoke Sound. This photo looks west across Colington Island to Albemarle Sound in the distance.*

(FIGURE 6)

topographic surface. The paleotopography and underlying geologic framework represent the inheritance that determines the entire character and health of each segment within the coastal zone.

Today's barrier islands and estuaries have migrated across and are perched on top of this ancient or paleo-land surface and associated drainage systems (Fig. 4). The character of this paleotopography and composition of underlying sediment units form the geologic heritage, the gene pool that determines the character of the coastal zone and its subsequent evolutionary history. Consequently, no two barriers are alike, nor are they equal in their inheritance or similar in their evolutionary development. Success or failure of many different aspects of "life at the edge of the sea" continues to be dictated by the realities that climate is still warming, glacial ice in polar regions is still melting, and sea level continues to rise.

The inherited paleotopography dictates the coastal system geometry, sand supplies to build the barrier islands, and shoreline recession or accretion rates. Many portions of the North Carolina coastal system are hung up on paleotopographic highs that form headlands composed of pre-existing rocks and sediments (Fig. 4A) and are exposed either on the beach or on the shoreface just below the ocean surface. Only a thin and highly variable amount of modern barrier island sand is perched upon these older geologic units that underlie the island and shoreface

(FIGURE 6) *Photographs show the character of sediment-poor, simple overwash barrier islands.* (PANEL A) *A 1998 oblique aerial photo of Madd Island, an undeveloped overwash barrier island. Notice the (1) large overwash fans of beach sand migrating over the back-barrier salt marsh, (2) vast and regularly flooded salt marsh, composed primarily of salt marsh cordgrass* (Spartina alterniflora), *and associated tidal creeks that essentially fill Topsail Sound, a narrow back-barrier estuary (3) dredged Intracoastal Waterway at the top of the photo, and (4) dark line of marsh mud and peat that crops out on the beach just above the breaker line.* (PANEL B) *A 1998 oblique aerial photo of Figure Eight Island, a developed overwash barrier island. The houses on Figure Eight Island were built either directly on a small beach berm or on back-barrier marsh filled with dredge spoil from the extensive channel dredging of back-barrier tidal channels. This private, overwash barrier island is severely sediment-starved and faces major long-term shoreline erosion problems.* (PANEL C) *A 1992 oblique aerial photo of the Rodanthe area, looking south, with the Atlantic Ocean on the left and Pamlico Sound on the right. The town of Rodanthe is located on a slightly wider portion of these Outer Banks. However, the shoreline is still receding, as indicated by the large sand overwash zone in the lower foreground, with numerous ocean-front houses in the process of being consumed by the encroaching ocean. Sound-side erosion is also a major problem on these islands because of the large and deeper-water character of Pamlico Sound.* (PANEL D) *A 1992 oblique aerial photo of the Buxton-Avon area, looking north, with the Atlantic Ocean on the right and Pamlico Sound on the left. The town of Avon is in the distance. This very narrow overwash barrier island segment has historically been the site of former inlets, with the last inlet forming here in 1962 during the Ash Wednesday Storm. This is also the location of North Carolina's most frequent "going-to-sea" coastal Highway 12. With almost every storm the road is overwashed and commonly destroyed, subsequently being rebuilt closer to the sound side. Notice the former "going-to-sea" highway coming out of Avon in the upper portion of the figure. In 1999, Hurricane Dennis took out the road in this photo, which was subsequently rebuilt directly on the Pamlico Sound shoreline. As this portion of the barrier island collapses, there will no longer be any place to move the road if shoreline recession continues. This figure is depicted on the north side of Buxton Woods in Figure 7B.*

(Figs. 5A and 5B). In part, composition of the older shoreface sediment units that are being excavated by wave energy determines the health of the associated barrier island. If the sediments are hard rocks such as limestone or cemented sandstone (Fig. 5A), there will be little to no new sediment contributed to the beach, and rates of shoreline recession will range from moderate to minimal. If the shoreface is composed of a soft mudstone (Fig. 5B), there will be no new sediment input onto the beach, leading to very high erosion rates and a rapidly receding shoreline. However, a shoreface consisting of unconsolidated sand will have a major input of new sediment to the beach that will minimize the relative rates of beach erosion and rates of shoreline recession.

Island segments that have relatively minor amounts of new sediment supplied to the beach form simple overwash-dominated barrier islands (Fig. 4A). These barrier segments are severely sediment-starved and therefore are extremely dynamic, with little potential for successful, long-term development. Examples of these types of barrier islands include the following: Masonboro, Figure Eight (Fig. 6B), Madd (Fig. 6A), and Topsail Islands; Core Banks; northeast Ocracoke Island, Buxton Overwash (Fig. 6D), and Pea Island (Fig. 6C).

However, island segments that have relatively large amounts of new sediment supplied to the beach produce large and complex barriers (Fig. 4B) consisting of multiple beach ridges,

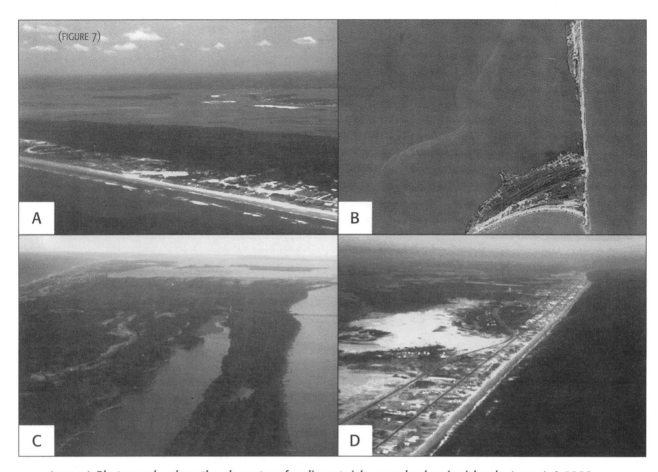

(FIGURE 7) *Photographs show the character of sediment-rich, complex barrier islands.* (PANEL A) *A 1982 oblique aerial photo of Emerald Isle on Bogue Banks, with Bogue Sound and the White Oak River estuaries in the background. Notice the very wide and high character of the complex barrier island that consists of a series of accretionary beach ridges covered with extensive maritime forest.* (PANEL B) *An EOSAT satellite image of Buxton Woods, a sediment-rich, complex barrier island built during prior sea-level conditions by the accretion of prograding beach ridges. This sediment-rich island is very high and wide and consequently contains a major maritime forest and fresh, ground-water aquifer. However, in spite of the previous sand-rich history of this island, today it is undergoing shoreline erosion due to ongoing sea-level rise. The simple overwash barriers that occur on both sides of Buxton Woods are sediment-starved, eroding severely, and in a serious state of collapse.* (photo from SPACESHOTS INC.) (PANEL C) *An oblique 1991 aerial photo of Southern Shores and Kitty Hawk, both of which occur in front of and in the maritime forest of Kitty Hawk Woods. The photo is looking south, with the Atlantic Ocean on the left. Kitty Hawk Bay is at the top of the photo, and Albemarle and Currituck sounds are on the right, with the causeway to Currituck County mainland separating the two sounds. Notice the linear, shore-parallel beach-ridge structures that were accreted during a previous period of the barrier island's history.* (PANEL D) *An oblique 1984 aerial photo of the Nags Head and Kill Devil Hills area. The photo is looking north, with the Atlantic Ocean on the right and Albemarle Sound on the left. From bottom to top on the barrier are the Seven Sisters Dunes, Jockeys Ridge, Nags Head Woods, and Kitty Hawk Bay. Notice the severe notch in an otherwise straight ocean shoreline, caused by increased erosion rates in the Kitty Hawk area and resulting in severe losses to houses, motels, and roads.*

back-barrier dune fields, and extensive maritime forests (Fig. 7). Because these islands are relatively sediment-rich, they tend to be more stable, and commonly have been the sites of habitation since humans first arrived on the North Carolina coast.

Complex barriers (Fig. 4B) form in three geologic settings where large sand supplies are periodically available for reworking into the coastal system. Islands that occur in association with older, sand-rich strata are actively being eroded and reworked into the new, adjacent barriers by the ongoing processes of storm action and sea-level rise. Examples of complex barrier islands that are products of this process include Bogue Banks (Fig. 7A), Bear Island, and Browns Island.

Complex islands develop from reworking delta deposits formed on the continental shelf at the mouths of major Piedmont-draining rivers during lower sea-level stands. The best examples occur at the earlier mouth of the Roanoke River and resulted in the creation of Colington Island, Kitty Hawk Woods (Fig. 7C), and Nags Head Woods (Fig. 7D) along with extensive back-barrier dune fields, including the Wright Brothers Monument, Run Hill (Figs. 5C and 5D), Jockeys Ridge (Fig. 7D), and the former Seven Sisters dune field. The islands immediately downstream of the cross-shelf cape shoals are commonly complex islands, consisting of very large volumes of sand with extensive maritime forests. Examples include Buxton Woods (Fig. 7B), Shackleford Banks, and Bald Head Island.

Barrier Island Dynamics and Human Modification

For centuries, the North Carolina barrier islands represented an extreme outpost of civilization—they were very high-energy, dynamic coastal systems that changed continuously through time and in response to highly changing energy conditions. Their raw and wild character has always attracted a small, independent component of human civilization, with small villages of hardy stock located mostly in maritime forests (Fig. 8A) or on the back side of the wider and more stable portions of the barriers (Figs. 9A and 10A). Other than a few islands near mainland urban areas (i.e., Wrightsville and Atlantic Beaches), the Carolina coast remained inaccessible except by boat until the first bridges were built in the early 1930s. Only then could outsiders readily visit the islands and begin to seriously consider the development potential of these remote places (Figs. 8B, 9B, and 10B).

The subsequent economic revolution could only happen along the oceanfront in response to a significant human manipulation of the natural beach system. Most barrier islands were characterized by very wide, low-sloping beaches dominated by storm overwash and little vegetation outside of the maritime forests (Figs. 8–10). The Wright brothers, as well as many others during the first thirty-five years of the twentieth century, inadvertently documented this characteristic in many photos of the northern Outer Banks (Fig. 11). However, the storm overwash characteristic of barriers was not conducive to economic development of these islands. Thus began the massive public works project of the late 1930s to create a continuous, vegetated, protective dune ridge from Virginia to Ocracoke through various programs, including the CCC and WPA.

Through these initial programs and the continuous need for reconstruction and maintenance of the dune ridges, we became experts in dune building along these wild islands (Figs. 12A and 12B). These sand ridges were perceived to be like the walls of a fort that would "protect" the

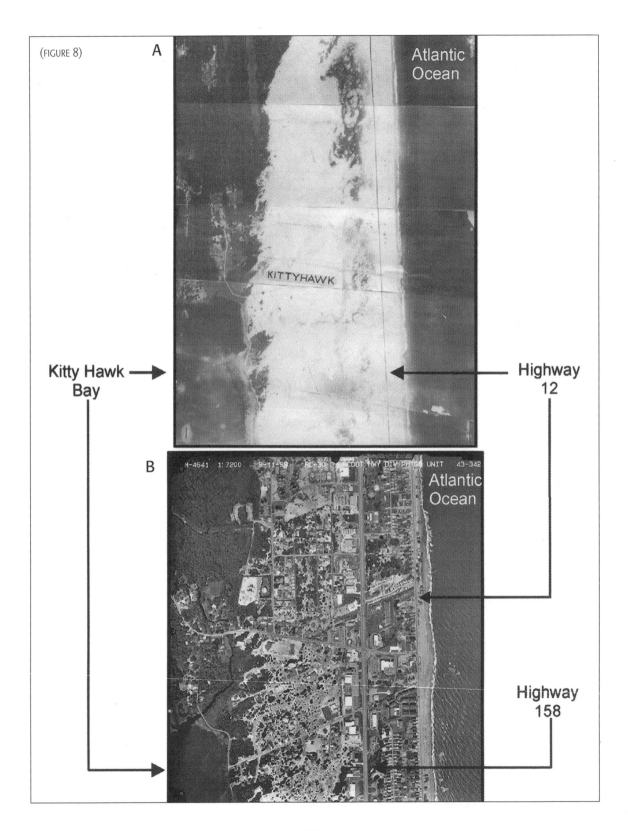

(FIGURE 8)

A

Atlantic Ocean

KITTYHAWK

Kitty Hawk Bay

Highway 12

B

M-4641 1:7200 9-11-98 RC-30 NCDOT HWY DIV PHTGM UNIT 43-342

Atlantic Ocean

Highway 158

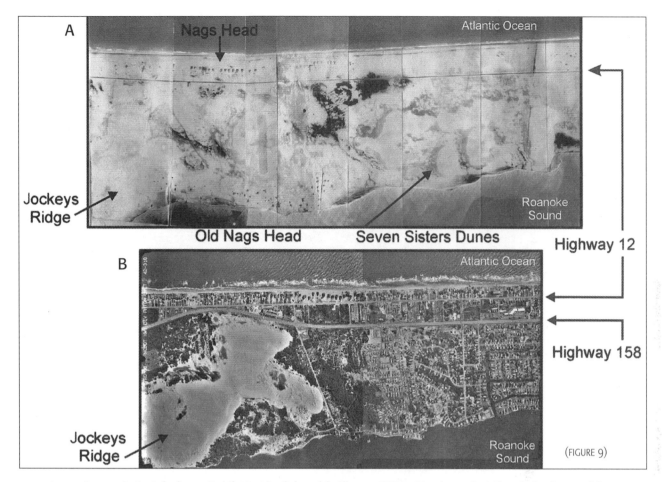

A Nags Head — Atlantic Ocean

Jockeys Ridge

Old Nags Head — Seven Sisters Dunes

Highway 12

Roanoke Sound

B Atlantic Ocean

Highway 158

Jockeys Ridge

Roanoke Sound

(FIGURE 9)

(FIGURE 8, PANEL A) *Aerial photo (April 1932) of the old village of Kitty Hawk nestled deeply in the maritime forest on an extremely wide portion of the barrier island. Notice the new Highway 12 that connects to the Currituck Peninsula bridge and was constructed just prior to this photograph.* (Photo courtesy of W. Birkemeier, U.S. Army Corps of Engineers, Field Research Facility, Duck, N.C.) (PANEL B) *Aerial photo (November 1999) of the same area showing the extreme levels of development and Highway 12 perched on the edge of the receding shore- line. Houses that used to exist east of Highway 12 have been lost to the ocean in response to average erosion rates of between four to eight feet per year.* (Photo courtesy of the N.C.D.O.T, Raleigh, N.C. Major differences occur in scales on the two photos.)

(FIGURE 9, PANEL A) *Aerial photo (April 1932) of Old Nags Head on Roanoke Sound showing Sound Side Road, Jockeys Ridge, and the first old homes built along the ocean front during the late 1800s. Notice the vast area of overwash without a natural barrier dune ridge. Also note the minimal amount of veg- etation that occurs in response to salt poisoning from the annual overwash processes.* (Photo courtesy of W. Birkemeier, U.S. Army Corps of Engineers, Field Research Facility, Duck, N.C.) (PANEL B) *Aerial photo (November 1999) of the same area showing the extensive barrier dune ridges, extreme development of vegetative cover in direct response to elimination of annual overwash processes, and extensive human development throughout the region, including the Seven Sisters dune field. Notice how the distance between the ocean and Highway 12 has narrowed due to the average rate of shoreline erosion of about four feet per year. This resulted in all the old houses in Panel A being moved back significant distances one or more times to their present position in Panel B.* (Photo courtesy of the N.C.D.O.T, Raleigh, N.C. Major differences occur in scales on the two photos.)

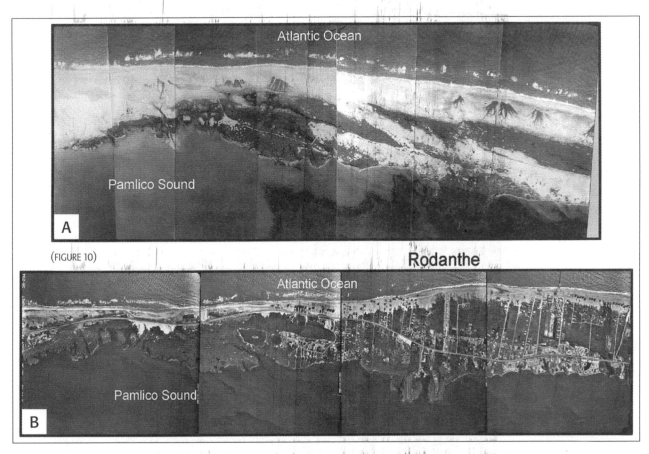

(FIGURE 10)

Rodanthe

(FIGURE 10, PANEL A) *Aerial photo (April 1932) shows the old village of Rodanthe on the Pamlico Sound side of a vast overwash barrier island without a natural barrier dune ridge. The minimal amount of vegetation occurs in direct response to saltwater inundation by the annual overwash processes.* (Photo courtesy of W. Birkemeier, U.S. Army Corps of Engineers, Field Research Facility, Duck, N.C.) (PANEL B) *Aerial photo (November 1999) shows the same area with an extensive barrier dune ridge, extreme development of vegetative cover in direct response to elimination of annual overwash processes, and high levels of human development. Notice that Highway 12 suffered a major overwash on the left side of the photograph. Also note the severe shoreline erosion and the great number of new houses that are now in the surf zone all along the coast due to the storms of 1999. The average erosion rate of sixteen feet per year has resulted in many houses lost to the ocean during storms.* (Photo courtesy of the N.C.D.O.T, Raleigh, N.C. Major differences occur in scales on the two photos.)

barrier islands from the angry sea and allow for their economic development (Fig. 12B). However, the dune ridges only provided a short-term insurance policy against small storms (Figs. 12C and 12D) and resulted in a false sense of security in challenging the oceanfront for the long term. The never-ending commitment to this "fort wall" has led to our headlong rush to change these barriers. We have redesigned the barriers from natural coastal features whose function was to act as energy-absorbing sponges between the ocean and land, to the economic backbone of a booming development and tourist industry. In the process, we severely modified the natural

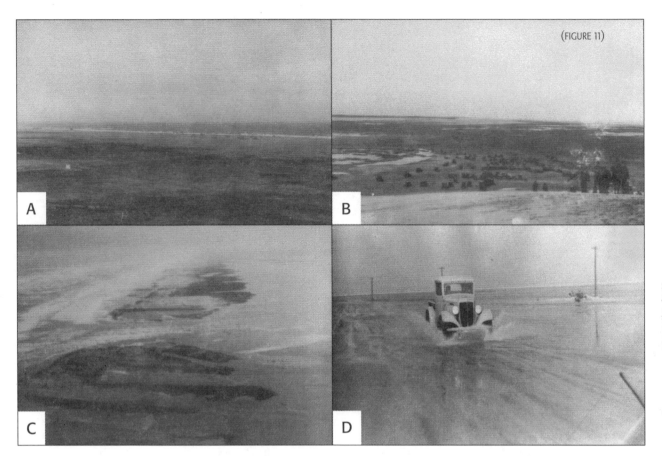

(FIGURE 11) *Photographs show the low overwash character of the natural barrier islands with a minimal vegetative cover limited by the regular overwash of salt water.* (PANEL A) *Photo is from the top of a sand dune looking towards the ocean shoreline, and shows only cars and people using the beach without structures or dune ridges and only a thin grassy vegetative cover.* (PANEL B) *Photo is from the top of a sand dune looking along the barrier toward other dunes in the background, separated by a thin grassy vegetative cover in the intervening flats. Photos A and B were taken by the Wright brothers between 1900 and 1911 in the vicinity of Kill Devil Hills.* (PANEL C) *Photo is an oblique aerial photo of storm over-wash during the 1962 Ash Wednesday nor'easter.* (PANEL D) *Photo is an automobile traveling along a sand road of the Outer Banks following a 1936 overwash event.* (All photos courtesy of the U.S. National Park Service, archives of the Cape Hatteras National Seashore, Manteo, N.C.)

dynamics that built these barriers and are essential for their long-term maintenance.

Through time the dune ridges produced only temporary fortification and rarely survived the bigger storms (Figs. 12C and 12D). However, after seven decades of maintenance and reconstruction of these dune ridges, there is a significant long-term price for this severe modification of natural processes. As global sea level continues to rise, the island shorelines have systematically receded and the beaches have become narrower and steeper. Also, dune ridges inhibited natural storm overwash processes, preventing sand buildup and marsh growth on the estuarine side of

(FIGURE 12) *Photographs show the process of construction and subsequent storm destruction of a barrier dune ridge.* (PANELS A & B) *Two types of shrubbery construction used to trap beach sand and build a barrier dune ridge in an effort to prevent the overwash process from inundating the barrier islands. The initial dune ridge was built during the late 1930s by Federal Government work programs (the CCC and WPA) and extended from the Virginia-North Carolina line to Ocracoke Inlet.* (PANELS C & D) *These show the destruction of the barrier dune ridge by the next series of storms and reestablishment of the natural overwash equilibrium profile. Thus began the ongoing war between the invading ocean and the barrier island developers.* (All photos courtesy of the U.S. National Park Service, archives of the Cape Hatteras National Seashore, Manteo, N.C.)

the overwash barriers. This has resulted in increased rates of estuarine shoreline erosion, particularly along the eastern shores of Pamlico Sound (Figs. 6C, 6D, and 10).

With ever-increasing levels of economic development, the dependency on building and maintaining dune ridges has created a drug-like addiction that has escalated to a declaration of war against the Atlantic Ocean by our tourist industry and political leaders (Figs. 13A and 13B). We now stand on a collision course in our attempt to maintain a stable, urban-type development on a set of high-energy dependent and extremely changeable barrier islands.

In a desperate effort to refortify our coast and hold the line in our war against the ocean, the towns, counties, and state and federal agencies representing about 120 miles of rapidly receding ocean shoreline are requesting financial support for immediate beach nourishment projects (Figs. 13C and 13D). If sand is available, the estimated initial project costs range from four to ten million dollars per mile, with the estimated fifty-year maintenance costs in excess of one billion dollars.

(FIGURE 13) *Photographs show the never-ending conflict between high-energy, mobile barrier islands responding to storms and rising sea level and the immobile and extremely fragile human structures fixed on the beach. (PANEL A) Close-up photo of storm waves overtopping the sandbag barricade built in a desperate effort to protect the "going-to-sea" coastal Highway 12 in the Pea Island overwash zone. This highway did "go to sea" shortly after this photo was taken and was rebuilt hundreds of feet to the west, where it continues to be overwashed with each major storm. (PANEL B) An ocean-front house in the surf zone at South Nags Head, as the shoreline recedes at an average rate of ten to fifteen feet per year in response to rising sea level. Notice the desperate effort of the owners to try to hold on one more season with a sea wall of giant sandbags. (PANEL C) A 1998 oblique aerial photo of a recently renourished, wide beach at Wrightsville Beach. This is a highly developed, sediment-starved, overwash barrier island that has experienced many beach nourishment projects since the 1930s. (PANEL D) A 1977 photo of the rock bulkhead at Carolina Beach, which protects the houses but has destroyed the beach. Consequently, this beach has a regular nourishment program that periodically and temporarily rebuilds the beach.*

The Drowned-River Estuarine System

The North Carolina estuaries are the drowned lowlands behind the barrier islands that are below sea level and are flooded by ocean waters. Where the lowlands are river valleys, the ocean has flooded up the rivers to the point where the valley bottom rises above sea level. The resulting shore-perpendicular estuaries are like long fingers reaching far into the heart of the coastal plain (Fig. 2). Two sources of water feed this estuarine system: fresh water flows down the rivers to the oceans and ocean water is pushed through the inlets by astronomical and storm tides. Consequently, these estuaries are great mixing basins where the two water masses interact to form the following salinity gradients: (1) fresh water in the upstream portions; (2) low-brackish water in the central regions; (3) high-brackish water in the outer estuaries and inlets; and (4) normal sea-water salinity in the offshore regions. Because of the differences in slope of the land and resulting barrier island and inlet systems in the two provinces, the estuarine mixing basins have dramatically distinct geometries, physical processes, and biological communities.

Back-Barrier Sounds

The back-barrier sounds of the northern province are medium to large, coast-parallel estuaries that include, from south to north, Core Sound, Pamlico Sound (which is the largest of all the estuaries), and Roanoke, Croatan, and Currituck sounds (Fig. 2). Only four inlets exist in over 190 miles of barrier islands, limiting the influence of oceanic water and processes to this estuarine system. In addition, there is a major input of fresh water from both Piedmont- and coastal plain-draining rivers. This results in very low-amplitude astronomical tides and highly variable salinities that range from fresh water to medium-brackish waters throughout extensive portions of these large water bodies. Only in the regions of direct oceanic influence around the inlets do the waters have regular astronomical tides and develop high-brackish salinities.

Core Sound has the highest salinities due to the presence of inlets at both ends and in the middle of the sound (Fig. 2), in combination with a minimum of fresh water input from rivers. Pamlico Sound ranges from high-brackish salinities around the three major inlets to medium- to low-brackish salinities along the western shores due to the high volume of fresh-water river discharge. Currituck Sound is totally fresh today due to the absence of inlets; however, historically there have been abundant inlets into Currituck Sound. Roanoke and Croatan sounds tend to have highly variable salinities that range from fresh to medium-brackish depending upon the amount of fresh water discharge and wind patterns.*

Because these sounds have relatively large surface areas with moderately uniform depths and no interior salt marshes, there is maximum response to waves and wind tides (Fig. 6C). Thus, the water is generally well-mixed by wind waves and currents as it sloshes back and forth in response to irregular and rapidly-changing weather events. Normal wind tides are minor (less than one foot) with storm tide amplitudes commonly up to three to five feet and, rarely, up to ten feet in response to major hurricanes. The direction, intensity, and duration of the wind determine the currents and tide levels. For example, a nor'easter that blows strongly for several days produces strong south-flowing currents. This will blow much of the water out of Currituck, Roanoke, and Croatan sounds (with three- to five-foot lower water levels) and produce flood conditions in southern Pamlico and Core sounds (with three- to five-foot higher water levels). This sloped water surface will hold as long as the wind continues to blow. As soon as the wind relaxes in intensity or shifts direction, the water flow responds immediately.

*For the effect of varying salinity levels on marine animals, see Lundie Spence's essay, "Estuaries: Where the River Meets the Ocean," in this volume, pp. 49–62, esp. p. 52.

(FIGURE 14) *Photographs show the character of eroding sediment-bank shorelines and the associated strandplain beaches along the North Carolina estuaries. Both the beach sand and the abundant downed trees are derived directly from the eroding sediment bank.* (PANELS A & B) *Two twenty-foot high sediment banks with associated strandplain beaches. In panel B, notice the slump blocks of sediment that are eroded during high wind tides when the water and associated waves directly attack the bluff. Under-cutting the bank results in the collapse of many trees that act as natural groins, trapping and holding the beach sand that is reworked from the slump blocks.* (PANEL C) *The seven-foot high sediment bank is actively being eroded and is rapidly encroaching upon this colonial farmhouse.* (PANEL D) *A three-foot high sediment bank has experienced significant erosion just since the farm crop was planted, as indicated by the truncated turning rows.*

On the other hand, during low-energy periods or seasons considerably less mixing occurs, resulting in much longer residence times for the estuarine water. Consequently, these back-barrier sounds tend to be irregularly flooded, wind-tide dominated coastal systems that are surrounded by scarped and rapidly eroding sediment banks (Fig. 14) and marsh shorelines (Fig. 15).

The back-barrier estuaries of the southern province are narrow, coast parallel estuaries that range from areas dominated by open water to areas dominated by salt marsh and tidal creek systems (Fig. 2). The widest systems contain small bodies of open water and include Back and

(FIGURE 15)

Bogue sounds south of Cape Lookout (Fig. 7A). As the estuarine system narrows in a southward direction, the size of the open-water bodies diminishes significantly to form Stump and Topsail sounds behind Topsail Island and the very small Middle and Myrtle Grove sounds behind Wrightsville Beach and Masonboro Island, respectively. In the latter regions and in the area south of Cape Fear, from Long Beach to Sunset Beach, the very narrow back-barrier estuaries are dominated by salt marshes that are highly dissected by tidal creeks (Figs. 6A, 6B, and 16A).

In the coastal segment from the southern portion of Carolina Beach to Fort Fisher (Fig. 2), the coast has no barrier islands. Here, older geologic units of the mainland form a subaerial headland with a strandplain shoreline eroded into the cemented sandstone units (Fig. 5B). Consequently, these outcropping rocks north of Fort Fisher form the only natural rocky beach in North Carolina. Because the shoreline is eroded into the mainland, there is no natural estuary and the Intracoastal Waterway occurs in a steep ditch cut through the upland.

The southern province is characterized by about eighteen inlets through the short, stubby barrier islands (Fig. 2). The combination of abundant inlets and few small coastal plain rivers draining into the coastal zone results in an estuarine system dominated by ocean water and ocean processes. Mixing within these estuaries is driven from the ocean by the highly regular astronomical tides (amplitude of three to five feet that increases southward), and associated tidal currents which rapidly mix the estuaries to form high-brackish waters.

(FIGURE 15) *Photographs show the character of estuarine salt marshes within the back-barrier sounds of the northern coastal province.* (PANEL A) *A low sediment-bank shoreline with a strandplain beach. This shoreline is somewhat protected from storm waves, allowing a fringing marsh to grow on portions of the strandplain beach. The marsh grasses are primarily black needlerush* (Juncus romerianus) *with some cordgrasses* (Spartina alterniflora *and* patens) *and other transition zone shrubs. Notice the large number of trees and stumps along the shoreline in the upper portion of the photo; this eroded debris trapped sand, producing the cuspate geometry and providing the shallow habitat for the marsh grasses to grow, which further trap sand. This is an excellent example of how both live and dead vegetation help protect sediment-bank shorelines on a short-term basis.* (PANEL B) *Photo of a vast, irregularly flooded, low-brackish black needlerush* (Juncus romerianus) *salt marsh. Notice the (1) abrupt shoreline that indicates an erosional bank that is severely undercut and collapsing, and (2) abundance of dead trees within the transition zone along the marsh perimeter. Upland trees around the marsh perimeter are drowning because of the rising water table, and are being replaced sequentially by the encroachment of transition zone and salt marsh habitats. Thus, marsh is being lost due to erosion on the seaward side and is being gained on the landward side as the marsh migrates upward and landward in direct response to ongoing sea-level rise.* (PANEL C) *Photo of slightly more protected, irregularly flooded, medium-brackish salt marsh dominated by black needlerush* (Juncus romerianus—gray brown) *with a thin fringe of salt marsh cordgrass* (Spartina alterniflora—bright green). *The dark green zones in the distance contain transition zone and upland vegetation due to slight increases in elevation from dredge spoil disposal.* (PANEL D) *Close-up photo of an eroding, irregularly flooded, medium-brackish salt marsh shoreline. This eroding peat bank consists of salt marsh cordgrass* (Spartina alterniflora) *fringing marsh in front of a slightly elevated dredge spoil bank covered with transition zone shrubbery. Notice the finger-like geometry along the marsh edge, resulting from active shoreline erosion from boat wakes in the adjacent dredged channel. The modern root mass binds the upper foot of marsh peat, forming a very tough mat; waves erode the soft portions of decomposing peat beneath the active root zone, severely undercutting the mat and causing it to flop in the waves until it breaks off in great chunks. These erosional processes along open marsh shorelines cause recession rates that commonly range up to many tens of feet per year.*

Because of their relatively small surface area, the water in these estuaries experiences minimal effects from waves and wind tides (Figs. 6A, 6B, 16A, and 16B). Consequently, large portions of the estuaries are dominated by sloped mudflats riddled with tidal channels and extensive salt marshes and oyster reefs (Fig. 16). These narrow estuaries are regularly flooded, tidal-current dominated coastal systems. Locally, these marshes have been highly modified by human activity, including an extensive network of dredged navigation channels and associated spoil islands, marsh drainage ditches for mosquito control, and landfill for development purposes.

Trunk Estuaries

Four major Piedmont-draining rivers flow into the northern province of the coastal zone (Fig. 1). The Chowan and Roanoke Rivers become the Albemarle Sound estuary, the Tar River becomes the Pamlico River estuary, and the Neuse River becomes the Neuse River estuary (Fig. 2). These brown-water, Piedmont-draining rivers form the major coast-perpendicular or trunk estuaries. The trunk rivers drain the Piedmont and Blue Ridge provinces, discharging large volumes of fresh water into the estuarine system with a significant load of sediment derived from the weathering and erosion of the upland red-clay soils.

(FIGURE 16) *Photographs show the character of back-barrier estuaries and associated salt marshes in the southern coastal province.* (PANEL A) *A 1998 oblique aerial photo of Middle Sound at high tide showing the extensive tidal creeks and associated regularly flooded, high-brackish marshes composed dominantly of salt marsh cordgrass (Spartina alterniflora). In the distance is Figure Eight Island, a private development built on a simple overwash barrier island with minimal sand and severe long-term problems.* (PANEL B) *A winter photo at low tide showing the regularly flooded, high-brackish marshes composed dominantly of salt marsh cordgrass (Spartina alterniflora) and associated tidal creeks and mud flats. The low-tide photo behind Sunset Beach shows the mudflat habitats and associated oyster reefs that occur within and adjacent to the tidal channels.* (PANEL C) *Close-up photo of a low-tide mudflat within the tidal channel and adjacent high-brackish, regularly flooded salt marsh composed of salt marsh cordgrass (Spartina alterniflora).* (PANEL D) *Close-up low-tide photo of prolific oyster reefs on a tidal channel mudflat behind Sunset Beach. In spite of the incredible abundance of oysters in this back-barrier sound, they are not edible and the oyster fishery is dead due to high levels of runoff from urban development, septic fields, and golf courses.*

The transition zone from river to estuary (Fig. 17A) occurs at the point where the river valley is flooded as it reaches sea level and riverine processes give way to estuarine processes. Due to the low-sloping land in the northern province, flooding occurs far upstream, producing the deeply embayed estuarine system with several thousands of miles of shoreline (Fig. 2).

Because the total volume of ocean flow through the four inlets is small and the fresh-water

(FIGURE 17) *Photographs show the character of drowned-river trunk estuaries and associated floodplain swamp-forest shorelines of the northern coastal province.* (PANEL A) *Oblique aerial photograph of the transition zone between Albemarle Sound and the Roanoke River and its swamp-forest floodplain. Notice the 1) farmland which occurs on the surrounding upland separated from the low floodplain by a high sediment bank and 2) shoreline erosion process by drowning which leaves cypress trees standing in the estuarine waters. The latter results as ongoing sea-level rise floods up the Roanoke River to produce the Albemarle Sound drowned-river estuary.* (PANEL B) *Vertical aerial photograph of the floodplain swamp-forest shoreline in Panel A with a few cypress trees left standing in the permanently flooded waters of Albemarle Sound.* (PANEL C) *Photograph of the floodplain swamp-forest shoreline in Panels A and B showing the few cypress trees left standing in the permanently flooded waters of Albemarle Sound.* (PANEL D) *Close-up photograph of the floodplain swamp-forest shoreline behind the drowned cypress trees in Panels A, B, and C.*

discharge is high, the trunk estuaries have low salinity. The Neuse and Pamlico River estuaries range from medium- to low-brackish salinity on the seaward side, and grade into low-brackish to fresh water in the landward direction. Albemarle Sound is almost totally fresh water due to the lack of oceanic influence. This lack of oceanic influence also results in the absence of regular astronomical tides and associated tidal currents.

Due to the large expanse of surface water in the trunk estuaries, wind and storm tides are important physical processes that irregularly mix the water column and set up the current patterns. Because these wind-tide fluctuations in water level are driven by the major weather patterns and individual storm events, these large embayed estuaries are irregularly-flooded, wave-dominated coastal systems that are only well-mixed during storms and the stormy seasons. Thus, during the hot and calm summer months, water temperature rises and unmixed water becomes stratified, causing significant chemical and biological consequences, including massive fish and clam kills.

Most rivers draining to the coast in the southern province are small black-water streams that discharge low volumes of fresh water (Fig. 2). These rivers carry relatively low sediment loads, but contain large quantities of organic components, giving the water the color of over-brewed tea. The one major exception to this is the Cape Fear River, which does drain the Piedmont (Fig. 1). Consequently, the Cape Fear River has a much larger river valley, a greater water discharge, and is a brown-water river due to the presence of sediment derived from erosion of the red-clay Piedmont soils.

The small trunk river valleys form a series of coast-perpendicular, drowned-river estuaries that include the North, Newport, White Oak, and New River estuaries (Fig. 2). These water bodies are much smaller than those in the northern province because they are coastal plain drainages with high land slopes. Also, the open-water bodies within the drowned-river estuaries are generally not broken by salt marshes and often have deeper water, causing wind waves and irregular wind tides to be important processes. Thus, the trunk estuaries tend to be irregularly flooded, wave-dominated coastal systems with shorelines characterized by eroding sediment banks (Fig. 14) and perimeter marshes (Fig. 15).

Many of these southern trunk estuaries are partially cut off from the back-barrier estuaries as a result of human activities. Construction of the Intracoastal Waterway and associated navigational channels resulted in an extensive network of dredge-spoil piles that greatly modified the water flow. In addition, some trunk estuaries have bridges across them which act as partial dams, further restricting current flow. These changes have dampened the oceanic influence, resulting in estuaries that are not as well mixed as the back-barrier estuaries and have a significantly decreased influence of regular astronomical tides. Consequently, over short distances the waters grade from high-brackish salinity at their mouths into low-brackish and fresh water away from the coast.

Tributary Estuaries

Flowing into the trunk estuaries is a network of tributary streams that are like the capillaries flowing into the arteries of the human circulation system (Fig. 2). The lower portion of each tributary valley is also drowned when it reaches sea level to form a generally coast-parallel estuary. In contrast to the trunk estuaries, the myriad of black-water tributary streams are all derived from the sandy coastal plain. These estuaries consist primarily of fresh water that is black due to the decomposition of organic matter derived in the upland swamps and pocosins that they drain.

Small tributary estuaries tend to have irregular riverine geometry and are characterized by low wind and wave energy. Thus, the shoreline is generally composed of either stable swamp

(FIGURE 18) *Photos of organic shorelines within tributary estuaries of both the northern and southern coastal provinces.* (PANEL A) *A typical swamp-forest shoreline that occurs within the floodplains of the fresh-water segments in the uppermost portions of the tributary estuaries. This is generally the beginning of the transition zone between the upstream riverine and the downstream estuarine systems. Notice that the minor rates of shoreline erosion take place through the permanent drowning of the floodplain trees.* (PANEL B) *As sea level rises and floods the former stream valley, the floodplain swamp-forest trees become stressed and die by permanent drowning. Notice that transition zone shrubbery and fresh-water marsh grasses readily replace the swamp-forest shoreline with a few remnant stumps exposed in the water.* (PANEL C) *Further seaward the swamp-forest zone continues to recede by drowning and is replaced by an expanding fresh-water to low-brackish marsh composed dominantly of giant cordgrass* (Spartina cynosuroides). (PANEL D) *Further down the tributary estuary, the water increases in salinity with a low-brackish marsh dominated by black needlerush* (Juncus romerianus).

forests in the upper reaches (Fig. 18A) or fringing fresh-water marsh (*Spartina cynosuroides* and *Phragmites*) that gradually replaces the drowning swamp forest habitat (Figs. 18B and 18C). The outer reaches are commonly filled with low-brackish salt marsh dominated by black needlerush (*Juncus roemerianus*) (Fig. 18D).

Tributary estuaries are smallest on the western or inner portions of the trunk estuaries and become generally larger in the eastward direction as the slope of the land approaches sea level (Fig. 2). Finally, on the eastern side where much of the land is now below sea level, the tributaries have flooded completely to form the very large back-barrier estuaries that include Core, Pamlico, Roanoke, Croatan, and Currituck sounds.

Estuarine Shorelines

All the North Carolina estuaries are products of the post-glacial rise in sea level that flooded the stream valleys of the coastal plain drainage system. The following shoreline types characterize the estuarine perimeters:

Sediment-Bank Shorelines (~33%)
    High Bank (Greater Than Five Feet Height)
    Low Bank (Less Than Five Feet Height)
Organic Shorelines (~67%)
    Swamp Forest (Fresh Water)
    Marsh Grass (Fresh, Brackish, and Salt Water)

Most sediment-bank shorelines are eroded into older sand and clay sediment units with thin and narrow sand beaches delicately perched along the water line to absorb the wave energy (Fig. 14). The shorelines dominated by vegetative growth (Figs. 15–18) are often characterized by peat sediment composed of organic matter with varying amounts of fine sand and mud deposits. The type of plants that dominate organic shorelines and their zonation patterns changes laterally as water salinity and tidal processes change.

Sediment-Bank Shorelines

Sediment-bank shorelines consist of a gently seaward-sloping, wave-cut platform below water level and the associated steeply-sloping, wave-cut scarp on the landward side of the beach (Fig. 14). The sand that forms the beach along the shoreline is derived from the erosion of the older units comprising the sediment bank. High-sediment banks range from five feet to greater than twenty feet in height, occur primarily in the westernmost portion of the estuarine system, are the least abundant type of shoreline, and are in the greatest demand for home-site development (Figs. 14A and 14B). Low-sediment banks (Figs. 14C and 14D) are less than five feet in height, are the most abundant shoreline type, and are dominant as the uplands slope eastward towards sea level. Protected segments of sediment-bank shorelines often contain small fringes of salt marsh (Fig. 15A) or remnant fringes of former riverine swamp-forests.

All sediment-bank shorelines are eroding, but at different rates depending upon their geographic location within the estuarine system and their exposure to wave energy. Erosion rates are extremely variable, ranging from a few feet per decade in the innermost trunk estuaries and small tributary estuaries to an average of three feet per year for exposed low sediment banks and marsh shorelines in the middle and outer estuarine reaches. Locally, the shorelines around Pamlico and Albemarle sounds have erosion rates that greatly exceed fifteen feet per year. Most shoreline erosion takes place in direct response to high-energy storms. Thus, the amount of recession at any location is quite variable from year to year. Because all beach sand on sediment-bank shorelines is derived from the erosion of adjacent sediment banks (Fig. 14), bulkheading the bank immediately terminates the sand supply and beach sands disappear.

Organic Shorelines

Swamp-forest shorelines are dominated by cypress, tupelo gum, and swamp maple trees (Figs. 17D and 18A) and occur within the fresh-water, riverine floodplains of the uppermost portions of trunk and tributary estuaries (Fig. 17A). As sea level rises, the riverine floodplain is permanently flooded and the trees drown (Figs. 18B and 18C). As the receding shoreline advances into the floodplain, a fringe of dead and dying trees is left behind in the water, producing one of the most characteristic and beautiful sights within the North Carolina estuarine system (Figs. 17A, 17B, and 17C).

Marsh shorelines occur throughout the estuaries and are dominated by emergent grasses with a transition zone to the adjacent upland composed of wax myrtle, marsh elder, and silverling (Figs. 15B and 18B). Within the inner estuarine system, fresh-water and brackish marshes may either occur as narrow fringing zones in front of wave-protected segments of sediment-bank shorelines (Figs. 18B and 18C) or may completely fill small tributary estuaries (Fig. 18D). Fresh-water marshes occur in the innermost riverine and estuarine regions and are dominated by cattails, bullrushes, reeds, and giant cordgrass (Figs. 18B and 18C). These marshes grade seaward into the brackish marshes that occur throughout most of the estuaries (Fig. 18D). In the outer estuarine regions of the northern province, where the land slope is minimal and approaches sea level, the brackish marshes form vast and spectacular wetland habitats (Figs. 15B and 15C). These irregularly-flooded brackish marshes are large, flat areas with few tidal channels, are dominated by a vast sea of gray-colored, black needlerush (*Juncus roemerianus*), and are rimmed with narrow fringes of bright green saltmeadow cordgrass (*Spartina alterniflora*) (Fig. 15C).

Organic shorelines of brackish marshes are characterized by thick beds of fairly pure peat, abruptly truncated by vertical and undercut scarps around the estuarine edge of the marsh (Fig. 15D). Brackish marshes are generally wave-dominated and are characterized by irregular storm-tide flooding. This situation generally causes the organic shorelines to be in an erosional mode. The outer marsh perimeter is often exposed to large stretches of open water with high wave energy, causing the peat shorelines to be actively eroded with undercut scarps that drop abruptly into three to eight feet of water. The landward side of these marshes is usually in a constructive mode, with the marsh migrating onto the adjacent upland areas as sea level rises (Fig. 15B).

The back-barrier estuaries of the southern province and areas around the inlets in the northern province are characterized by high-brackish salinity and are regularly flooded by astronomical tidal currents (Fig. 16A). Sandy peats of the salt marsh growing above mean-tide level (Figs. 16B and 16C) characterize the organic shorelines. Bright green salt marsh and salt meadow cordgrasses (*Spartina alterniflora* and *Spartina patens*, respectively) form the dominant vegetation in these salt marshes. Extensive low-sloping mudflats and sandflats (Figs. 16B and 16C), covered with vast reefs of oysters (Fig. 16D), extend below mean-tide level and into the adjacent tidal channels. The marsh vegetation grows on the upper portions of these low-sloping ramps, where it actively traps sediment and builds the shoreline out into the estuary.

Loving Our Coastal System to Death

Natural and human-induced hazards abound in the coastal region. Pollution is the most sinister of hazards that threaten both human health and the natural habitats we proclaim to love (Figs. 19A and 19B). In addition, if you live and work in the coastal zone you face an extremely high possibility of property loss resulting from flooding, shoreline erosion, and other storm-induced factors (Figs. 13A and 13B). The burgeoning populations and exploding community development negatively impact the coast and take their cumulative toll on the health of the entire system. The limited resources within our coastal system make this an earth habitat that truly does have "limits to growth."

Population and pollution are wed in an intimate relationship. Demographic increases lead to increases in human-produced waste, much of which is discharged into our waterways. Today there are thousands of NPDES (National Pollution Discharge Elimination System) point sources that discharge industrial and municipal waste into our North Carolina rivers and estuaries. In theory, these point sources discharge known volumes and compositions of waste material. In reality, the composition is poorly known for anything other than a handful of components that are regulated and monitored, including oxygen, chloride, nutrients such as phosphorus and nitrogen, and organic components such as fecal coliform along with temperature, pH, turbidity, and a few others. Occasionally, known contaminants such as dioxin, mercury, lead, zinc, and copper are required to be monitored by an individual discharger. However, it is rare that such waste materials are actually regulated. Otherwise, almost every chemical and compound used in our industrial society has the potential of being discharged into our "sewers," which are the rivers and estuaries of North Carolina. This approach is acceptable because society believes that "dilution is the solution to pollution." Toxic materials are diluted to small enough concentrations to make that particular component appear "harmless." But this may not be the case. If the pollutant is chemically active, it may be reconcentrated by either the sediments or organisms within the estuaries.

This is only a part of the problem with pollution. Point source discharges represent approximately one third (municipal, domestic, and industrial point sources) of the total pollution load to the estuarine system. The largest source of contaminants is the additional two thirds that comes from non-point sources, of which little is known. Sources of nonpoint discharges are extremely varied in space, time, volume, and chemical composition and include agriculture, silvaculture, urban stormwater runoff, hog farms, golf courses, groundwater discharge associated with historic waste dump sites and landfills, land and shoreline erosion, and atmospheric fallout. In addition, many of the coastal zone farmlands are severely dissected by drainage ditches, swamp forests are drained, and associated streams are channelized. Major drainage modifications represent standard land-use practice but they have devastating effects upon both the rivers and downstream estuarine water bodies. Stormwaters carrying sediment and chemical pesticides, herbicides, and fertilizers are shunted directly off the fields through ditches and into the streams and estuaries with minimum natural filtration.

The estuaries are settling basins that receive the riverine sediment, organic matter, and human waste and chemicals resulting from agriculture, urbanization, and industrialization throughout the associated drainage basins. All of these materials accumulate within the settling

(FIGURE 19) *Photographs show the alteration and slow death of our estuarine system in direct response to the rapid economic growth and development of the North Carolina coastal region.* (PANEL A) *The all-too-frequently-seen warning sign of the North Carolina Division of Marine Fisheries stating that shellfish in this region are contaminated and should not be eaten. The contamination comes from the numerous marinas, dense use of septic systems, ever-increasing amounts of stormwater runoff from expanding urban development, agricultural land, and golf courses, and continued discharge of chemical pollutants into our waterways.* (PANEL B) *The increasing frequency of fish kills containing significantly increased numbers of diseased fish. The rapid increase in numbers of diseased fish reflects the rapid decline in estuarine water quality.* (PANEL C) *Oblique aerial photograph of North Carolina's newest super-highway bridge across the Neuse River estuary at New Bern. This spaghetti-bowl highway system might be beautiful in Raleigh or Atlanta, but here it is a symbol reflecting the pressure that the population explosion places upon the limited resources of our coastal system.* (PANEL D) *Photograph of the desperate efforts of shoreline landowners to build rock and wooden bulkheads to protect their eroding estuarine sediment-bank shorelines.*

basin with different residence times and pathways through the system. Some waste material remains and becomes part of the estuarine dynamics, where it impacts the sediment and water quality and ultimately stresses the organisms living within this ecosystem (Figs. 19A and 19B). Some of the waste is ephemeral and eventually passes on through the estuaries and into the oceanic system, as it is intended to do. The rates, pathways, and effects of these contaminants are different in the northern and southern provinces and for each type of estuarine system within each province.

Another important effect of human development upon the coastal system is habitat modification in direct response to rapid population growth and rates of development within our coastal system. Some of the greatest population growth rates in North Carolina are occurring within our coastal counties, leading to an explosion of the urbanization process throughout the coastal zone. The unprecedented rate of new four-lane bridge construction (Fig. 19C) leads to ever-increasing growth and development and increases the pressure on already over-burdened water supplies and sewage disposal systems. This growth, intimately intertwined with a booming tourist industry, causes major cumulative wetland losses and habitat modifications. Cleared maritime forests, bulkheaded shorelines (Fig. 19D), dredged shallow-water habitats, channelized wetlands, bulldozed dune fields, and paved parking lots all modify the land surface, alter the drainage, and result in increased contaminants moving into the adjacent coastal waters.

Conclusion

The coastal system is not fragile—it is a high-energy dependent system that is characterized by environmental extremes and reliant upon storm events to maintain the overall health of the natural system. Rather, it is the fixed human superstructure that we superimpose upon this dynamic system that is fragile. The fact is, there is no guaranteed permanency to any characteristic or feature within the North Carolina coastal system. The early settlers of our coastal system understood this. However, modern society has forgotten the environmental constraints of this dynamic and changeable coastal system in our headlong rush to transform it into a replica of inland "urban development"!

RECOMMENDATIONS FOR FURTHER READING

Barnes, Jay. *North Carolina's Hurricane History*. Chapel Hill/London: UNC Press, 1995.

Bush, David M., William J. Neal, and Orrin H. Pilkey. *Living by the Rules of the Sea*. Durham, NC: Duke Univ. Press, 1996.

Cleary, William J., and Tara P. Marden. *Shifting Shorelines: A Pictorial Atlas of North Carolina Inlets*. Raleigh, NC: NC Sea Grant Publication, (1999): UNC-SG-99-04.

Frankenberg, Dirk, ed., *Exploring North Carolina's Natural Areas: Parks, Nature Preserves, and Hiking Trails*. Chapel Hill/London: UNC Press, 2000.

_____. *The Nature of the Outer Banks: Environmental Processes, Field Sites, and Development Issues, Corolla to Ocracoke*. Chapel Hill/London: UNC Press, 1995.

_____. *The Nature of North Carolina's Southern Coast: Barrier Islands, Coastal Waters, and Wetlands*. Chapel Hill/London: UNC Press, 1997.

Godfrey, Paul J. and Melinda M. Godfrey. *Barrier Island Ecology of Cape Lookout National Seashore and Vicinity, North Carolina*. National Park Service Scientific Monograph Series, No. 9, Washington DC: U.S. Government Printing Office, 1976.

Hayes, Miles O. "General morphology and sediment patterns in tidal inlets." *Sedimentary Geology* 26 (1980), 139–156.

Kaufman, Wallace and Orrin H. Pilkey. *The Beaches are Moving: The Drowning of America's Shoreline*. Durham, NC: Duke Univ. Press, 1979.

Pilkey, Orrin H., William J. Neal, Stanley R. Riggs, et al. *The North Carolina Shore and its Barrier Islands: Restless Ribbons of Sand*. Durham, NC: Duke Univ. Press, 1998.

Riggs, Stanley R. *Estuarine Shoreline Erosion in North Carolina: Cause and Effect*. Raleigh, NC: NC Sea Grant Publication, (2002): UNC-SG-01-11.

Schoenbaum, Thomas J. *Islands, Capes, and Sounds of the North Carolina Coast*. Winston-Salem, NC: John F. Blair, Publisher, 1982.

Stick, David. *The Outer Banks of North Carolina, 1584–1958*. Chapel Hill/London: UNC Press, 1958.

Archaeology and Ancient Cultures at the Edge of the Sea

— I. Randolph Daniel, Jr. —

When discussing the early history of our state, the subject invariably turns to the fabled "Lost Colony." The mystery surrounding the disappearance of the sixteenth-century English colonists on Roanoke Island endures centuries later. The settlement's failure notwithstanding, the English venture is significant because it marks the beginnings of North Carolina's written history. The various records associated with that expedition—including Thomas Hariot's earlier written descriptions and John White's detailed watercolors—provide first-hand accounts that historians use to chronicle early English experiences on the North Carolina coast. But what about the rest of the story? What of prior attempts at colonization that *were* successful over ten millennia earlier? Certainly those efforts—and descriptions covering over ten thousand years of native lifeways in the state—merit equal attention, yet no literary accounts of that story remain for historians to chronicle. Rather, the task of reconstructing the state's unwritten history falls to archaeologists. This can only be done through the careful excavation and thoughtful interpretation of the buried material remains that were discarded, lost, or left behind by the state's earliest inhabitants.

What follows, then, is a broad outline of that unwritten past as it relates to eastern North Carolina. Much of what I recount is drawn from the archaeology done by East Carolina University (ECU) since the archaeology program was founded in 1970. Consequently, I draw primarily upon the work done by my colleagues David Phelps, Professor Emeritus, and John Byrd, formerly of the Anthropology Department. I also draw upon some of my own research, although I am a relative newcomer to conducting archaeology in the coastal plain. By emphasizing ECU's contributions to coastal plain prehistory, I do not mean to downplay the work done by the state's other professional archaeologists. Driven by historic preservation legislation, archaeologists employed by state and federal agencies, as well as those working in the private sector, have done much important archaeology in the region. Likewise, because my emphasis is on the state's prehistory, I have not included the significant strides made in historical archaeology by my colleague Charles Ewen at ECU. I simply wish to emphasize the seminal role that ECU has played in developing the region's prehistory by highlighting some of the more important projects we have undertaken.

Most archaeologists divide the state's prehistory into four major temporal units that include the Paleoindian, Archaic, Woodland, and Contact periods. This sequence follows cultural trends marking important changes in prehistoric lifeways seen elsewhere in the Southeast. Adhered to here, this sequence allows the reader to relate eastern North Carolina's prehistory to the "big picture" of southeastern United States prehistory.

Paleoindian Period (11,000–8000 B.C.)

The Paleoindian Period is generally believed to mark the earliest widespread presence of humans in North Carolina, or North America for that matter: somewhere around 13,000 years ago. Exactly when humans first entered North America is a subject of considerable debate among archaeologists. In fact, recent finds in the southeastern United States are leading some archaeologists to believe that the peopling of North America may have occurred several thousand years earlier than originally thought. These claims are very controversial, however, and what implications, if any, they have for North Carolina is unclear. In any case, these first colonizers likely shared hunting and gathering lifeways, living in small bands composed of a few families. Specific adaptations most likely varied regionally across the continent, and probably involved frequent residential movements in search of various resources.

Paleoindian sites were first discovered in the Southwest some eight decades ago, where archaeologists uncovered stone spear points associated with the bones of now-extinct Ice Age mammals such as mammoth, mastodon, and bison. These locations have been interpreted as "kill sites" documenting the hunting practices of early Native Americans. As the term Ice Age implies, both animals and people would have lived in environmental conditions much different than today's. Vast ice sheets covered a large portion of the northern continent, influencing human adaptations. In North Carolina, for example, climatic conditions would have been cooler and moister than at present. Likewise, the state's earliest inhabitants would have seen a much different landscape than currently exists. In particular, significantly lower sea levels would have exposed much of what is now the continental shelf, extending the state's shoreline several miles to the east.* In addition, rather than the oak and pine forest that dominates the region today, a mixed hardwood forest existed, dominated by beech and hickory but including a mix of other hardwood species.

Unfortunately, no Paleoindian archaeological sites *per se* have been excavated in the state. Rather than sites, Paleoindian remains occur as isolated surface finds in the form of diagnostic stone spear points referred to as "fluted points." These artifacts are similar to those found in the Southwest mentioned above and are characteristic of the Paleoindian Period across the entire continent. Fluted points are finely flaked into a lanceolate shape usually three to five inches in length. A basal "flute" is their distinguishing attribute. This flute forms a channel or groove that

*For more information on the movement over time of North Carolina's dynamic shoreline, see Stanley R. Riggs's essay, "Life at the Edge of North Carolina's Coastal System: The Geologic Controls," in this volume, pp. 63–95, esp. pp. 68–75.

runs the length of the point base, presumably to facilitate hafting the point to a spear shaft by thinning its base.

Since I arrived at ECU, my research has been geared toward finding evidence of the state's earliest inhabitants on the coast. This research strategy has included a two-pronged attack: the search for a Paleoindian site containing a concentration of artifacts that would lend themselves to archaeological excavation, coupled with a statewide study of the distribution of fluted points. Thus far, I have had the most success with the latter approach, recording information regarding fluted points across the state in both private and institutional collections. To date, I have recorded over 200 specimens recovered from sixty-five counties. Forty-eight of these artifacts were recovered from coastal plain counties. The distribution of fluted points in the eastern part of the state is part of a geographic pattern that includes a large concentration of points, covering most of the Piedmont and inner coastal plain. This concentration can be explained, at least in part, by the presence of high-quality stone quarries along the eastern edge of the Piedmont. One implication of this pattern is that Paleoindian settlement in the state may have necessitated regular use of these quarries.

Another interesting fact emerges concerning Paleoindian settlement. Studying the distribution of Paleoindian points and the stone type from which they were manufactured suggests that Paleoindian mobility covered large portions of the state and adjacent regions. That is, fluted points found in the coastal plain are commonly made from rhyolite, a stone that outcrops in the Piedmont rather than the coastal plain.

Moreover, an appreciable number of points are made from various types of chert, a stone type that does not appear to have been obtained from within the state. Assuming that these occurrences track the movement of stone obtained directly from its source to locations where it was discarded, then the use of these stone types as raw material suggests that the annual rounds of Paleoindian groups occupying the coastal plain also included at least portions of the Piedmont, as well as areas outside what is now North Carolina. This might make particular sense as

North Carolina fluted point. (courtesy of Phelps Archaeology Laboratory, East Carolina University)

the coastal plain is a relatively poor source for workable stone—an important resource for tools among these prehistoric hunter-gatherers. Such high mobility is not unusual, given ethnographic accounts of hunter-gatherers who covered hundreds of square miles annually. This is also a trend seen in the archaeological record on a continent-wide basis for the Paleoindian Period.

Beyond that, the presence of fluted points in the coastal plain is typical of elsewhere in the state, consisting of a few specimens recovered as surface finds. Consequently, the rareness and context of these artifacts provide precious little information about prehistoric daily life during this remote period. This is a common archaeological pattern across virtually the entire Southeast, leading some scholars to suggest that Paleoindian folk were true ecological foragers, moving

East Carolina University excavations at the Barber Creek site. (photo by Randy Daniel)

across the landscape in such low population densities and with site occupations so short that they resulted in only ephemeral remains. On the other hand, some archaeologists temper this interpretation with the archaeological adage that "to find old sites one needs to find old dirt," suggesting that we might not be looking in the right places. That is, our efforts should be focused in locations where geological conditions preserved ancient sediments. If one is looking for a needle in a haystack, one needs to be sure to start with the right haystack.

I have been particularly mindful of this adage in my search for a location with buried Paleoindian remains. With regards to this, I am particularly excited about the prospects of finding such a "haystack" along Barber Creek, a tributary of the Tar River where we conducted preliminary excavations in the summer of 2000. Our excavations suggest that sediments have been accumulating almost continuously in this location for over 10,000 years. At least two major occupations are stacked some two feet deep in these sediments, including archaeological remains dating to the Woodland and Archaic periods. While other such "stratified" sites have been located in the Piedmont, this is the first time such a site has been identified in the coastal plain. Of significance here, however, is some tantalizing evidence of a deeper occupation at three feet below the surface. At least two small stone scrapers recovered at that level are suggestive—though not conclusive—of a Paleoindian occupation at Barber Creek. Two lines of evidence tentatively support this age assignment. First, although their recovery is not as convincing as would be that of a fluted point, the artifact forms are similar to those found in Paleoindian stone tool assemblages from elsewhere in the country. Second, these artifacts were recovered about one foot below the Archaic component, which was radiocarbon dated to around 8000 B.C. Presumably, artifacts coming from well below that level would fall into the Paleoindian time range. In any event, I am cautiously optimistic about the site's potential to yield evidence about the state's first colonists. Much more excavation is needed to confirm my expectations, but my students have strong backs and will work surprisingly hard in return for a few college credits. I eagerly anticipate our return to Barber Creek this summer (2002).

Archaic Period (8,000–1000 B.C.)

While Paleoindian points are exceedingly rare in the coastal plain, spear points from the subsequent Archaic Period are recovered in much greater numbers. In fact, one can walk virtually any plowed field in the coastal plain with a nearby water source and find stone points or other stone artifacts dating to the Archaic Period. Several thousand Archaic points, for example, exist in the archaeology collections at ECU. These artifacts have been recovered primarily as a result of the numerous archaeological surveys conducted by ECU over the last thirty years in the northern coastal plain.

The Archaic Period encompasses the onset of more modern climatic conditions. Consequently, Archaic peoples likely settled into environmental conditions similar to contemporary ones and continued a hunting-gathering way of life adapted to more modern habitats. By convention, the several thousand years that encompass the Archaic are divided into three intervals, appropriately termed Early, Middle, and Late. These three subdivisions are identified in the archaeological record primarily by changes in the form of stone points. We know this as a result of excavations that took place several decades ago at a handful of sites in the Piedmont. A composite sequence was put together at these sites where deep archaeological deposits accumulated as a result of intermittent occupations over several thousand years. Careful excavation allowed archaeologists to identify the layered nature of these sites, documenting the order in which point styles changed over time. Recovered from the deepest level at one site, a lanceolate-like form exhibiting an "eared" base reflects a "transitional" point style marking the end of the Paleoindian Period and the beginning of the Archaic. Subsequently, notched-base point styles developed. Various types of stemmed base point types representing the Middle and Late Archaic mark the latter portion of the period. Reasons for these changes remain unclear, but to some extent the changes probably reflect how hunting weapons were used. For instance, the shift from lanceolate to notched forms is thought to reflect a change from thrusting spears to a smaller spear form propelled by an "atlatl"—a hand-held spear-throwing device. Likewise, some archaeologists claim that the change reflects an increased need for these points to function as knives as well as projectiles.

In any case, this typological and chronological framework has allowed archaeologists to address additional issues like Archaic settlement practices in the region. A recent study by one of my graduate students provides a good example of this research. John Cooke examined Archaic land-use practices by analyzing the distribution of over 4,000 points recovered from over 600 sites in twenty-seven counties in the northern coastal plain. Although some settlement differences were noted throughout the Archaic, Cooke noted three general patterns in the data. First, little difference existed in the distribution of Archaic point types and their stone material type both along and across the major river drainages of the northern coastal plain. Second, high frequencies of points made from stone quarried in the Piedmont were present in the coastal plain. These two patterns were interpreted to reflect that Archaic settlement was not confined to any particular drainage, nor was it confined to the coastal plain. Settlement mobility likely included regular movement between the Piedmont and coastal plain, traveling along or crossing drainage basins. A third pattern in the data indicated that almost half of the points were concentrated in counties along the Fall Line. Point frequencies declined considerably toward the coastal counties, however. Assuming that point frequencies reflect intensity of land use, then this pattern suggests yet another facet about Archaic settlement strategies. Might the Fall Line represent some physiographic ecotone between the Piedmont and coastal plain, making it a strategic location for these prehistoric hunter-gatherers to use? For instance, higher point densities might reflect intensively occupied Fall Line camps that provided equal access to resources in either the Piedmont or coastal plain. Alternatively, the Fall Line location simply may have been revisited more frequently, rather than more intensively, as groups moved back and forth along drainages between the Piedmont and coastal plain. Only extensive excavations aimed at appropriate sites will resolve this question.

This latter fact points to a major deficiency in our knowledge of coastal plain prehistory. As is the case with the Paleoindian Period, virtually no attention has been paid to locating and excavating sites with significant Archaic remains in the region. While work like Cooke's is important and provides us with a "big picture" perspective, extensive excavations at sites with sufficient Archaic remains are needed to allow us to fully understand Archaic adaptations. And this brings me back to Barber Creek. Even with our limited excavations thus far, we have identified an Early Archaic level at Barber Creek uncovering stone points, scrapers, and other artifacts. Furthermore, to my knowledge the radiocarbon date mentioned above represents the oldest such date yet obtained from an archaeological site in North Carolina. Future work will be aimed at expanding the excavations to acquire a larger sample of artifacts that might provide clues as to the range of activities undertaken at the site. I am confident that much remains to be uncovered at Barber Creek that will help us begin to better understand Archaic adaptations in the coastal plain.

By about 5,000 years ago some significant cultural changes were taking place around the Southeast with respect to subsistence strategies, settlement practices, and technology. For instance, fishing and shell-fishing became major food resources in the Late Archaic. At this point in time, large sites in the form of freshwater mollusk middens were located along inland waterways like the Savannah, Tennessee, and Green rivers. Sites like these marked a trend toward more sedentary occupations and population increase around the Southeast. Technologically, stone vessels made their appearance, carved from steatite, or soapstone—a relatively soft stone with a heat-retention quality that made it an ideal raw material for making containers used to cook soups and stews. These containers presaged the appearance of ceramic vessels during the following Woodland Period. Other economic changes included increased harvesting of seedy plants like sunflower, maygrass, and chenopodium, marking the beginnings of serious attempts at plant cultivation.

Again, in the absence of excavated data, it is hard to assess to what degree all of these cultural changes were present in the North Carolina coastal plain. Survey data suggest that population increased during the latter portion of the Archaic. Larger sites appear to be present along the mouths of major rivers, although none of these exhibits extensive shellfish middens—shell heaps representing the remains of freshwater mollusks found along other southeastern United States rivers. Nevertheless, we can postulate that river resources such as fish, turtles, and perhaps waterfowl were important seasonal resources. And while no plant remains have been recovered from Late Archaic contexts in the region, the presence of large stone axe heads—that occasionally turn up in plowed fields in eastern North Carolina along with stone points—indirectly hints at the beginnings of horticulture. These large chipped-stone and ground-stone ax heads display wide grooves to facilitate hafting. As such, they were undoubtedly used for heavy-duty chopping tasks. Clearing fields for cultivation would be consistent with the first appearance of these axes in the archaeological record.

Woodland Period (1000 B.C.–ca. A.D. 1550)

The Woodland Period is generally viewed as a time when peoples throughout the eastern United States experienced increased sedentism, population growth, and political complexity. Like the Archaic Period, the Woodland Period is divided into three intervals termed Early, Middle, and Late. At the beginning of the period, people are assumed to have been living in small groups, loosely bound by collective rituals associated with mound burial. By A.D. 1000, some parts of the region experienced densely populated villages associated with large earthen mounds constructed for use as house platforms as well as burial purposes by hereditary elites. Increased inter-tribal conflicts also accompanied these cultural changes. Food collecting was now replaced with food production: corn agriculture dominated subsistence practices across much of the region. The degree to which the native groups in North Carolina participated in these trends varied across the state. Mound building, for example, appears to have been rarely performed in eastern North Carolina and then restricted to the southern coastal plain. Furthermore, by the end of the period, eastern North Carolina exhibited cultural adaptations unique to the coastal region.

Archaeologically, the Early Woodland is marked by the appearance of sand-tempered ceramics, estimated as having occurred around 1000 B.C. in the coastal plain. Pottery studies, in fact, have dominated much of the archaeological research conducted by ECU—and for good reason. Pottery fragments are ubiquitous on archaeological sites and we have found that they are useful markers of temporal change. These fragments were part of vessels used originally for cooking and storage; they were made by hand-coiling strips of clay mixed with some additive referred to as temper, followed by stamping the exterior pot surface with a paddle to bind the coils together just prior to firing. In particular, archaeologists have noted that temper and surface impressions left by the paddles are particularly sensitive indicators of time.

Using these attributes, by the mid-1980s David Phelps had devised a rough ceramic chronology for eastern North Carolina. Broadly speaking, temper can be used to sort pottery according to the following sequence: a coarse

Woodland Period pottery from the Barber Creek site: Fabric-impressed pottery (top row); cord-marked pottery (bottom row).
(photo by Randy Daniel)

103

sand temper during the Early Woodland, a "grog" (fired clay or crushed pottery bits) temper during the Middle Woodland, and a crushed shell temper during the Late Woodland. Furthermore, exterior surface treatments roughly correlate with temper as well, particularly since the paddles were often wrapped with materials that left distinctive impressions like cordage, nets, and fabrics. More rarely, the paddle was unwrapped and exhibited various carved designs that were stamped directly onto the surface of the pot. Again, generally speaking, pottery with cord-marked surfaces tends to occur early in the Woodland Period, while fabric-impressed surfaces tend to predominate in the latter portion of the period. Unfortunately for archaeologists, however, tempers and surface treatments are not exclusively associated with specific periods of time. For example, sand tempering and fabric impressing may have been present to some degree in both the Early and Middle Woodland in the northern coastal plain. Further excavation at appropriate sites will be necessary to sort out this problem.

Indeed, the past decade has seen a renewed interest among my colleagues in refining our understanding of pottery types in the region. To illustrate, seven of eight articles in a 1999 issue of the journal *North Carolina Archaeology* are devoted to pottery taxonomy in the eastern part of the state. At the risk of belaboring the point, it does provide an example of how archaeologists try to make sense of archaeological data.

Beyond pottery studies, we can only make broad statements about Woodland lifestyles during the first two millennia of the period, suggesting that the Late Archaic subsistence practices of hunting, gathering, and fishing continued as important food collecting practices. Although food cultivation begins to take on a more important role elsewhere in the Southeast, we cannot at present evaluate to what degree plant cultivation was important in the coastal plain during this time. Much of our problem stems from the lack of excavated sites with clearly defined Early and Middle Woodland occupations. A handful of sites in the northern coast have received only partial excavation by ECU archaeologists, both inland along the Roanoke River and on the Outer Banks. What the evidence from these sites suggests is that Middle Woodland folk were settling into more sedentary villages along mainland waterways while spending at least a portion of the year on the coast collecting shellfish. Inland riverine sites are presumed to be related to the increased importance of domesticated plants as a food source.

We know much more about the latter portion of the Woodland Period in the northern coastal plain, largely because of the relatively greater amount of attention it has received archaeologically. Distinct material differences that date just before A.D. 1000 appear in the archaeological record across the coastal plain. These material traits included differences in ceramic traditions, settlement and subsistence practices, and burial customs that are believed to reflect an increased regionalization in cultural adaptations. In addition to the division of the coastal plain into northern and southern regions, a further distinction can be made: the northern coastal plain can be further subdivided into the inner and outer coastal plain. These geographic distinctions coincide with historically recognized native peoples. In particular, Algonkian-speaking groups occupied the tidewater zone of the northern coast, while the Iroquoian-speaking Tuscaroras inhabited the inner coastal plain. Similarly, the southern region is seen as the territory of the historic Siouan-speaking tribes. At ECU, our archaeological program has concentrated on Algonkian- and Tuscarora-related sites.

It is not difficult to find evidence of late prehistoric settlements along the northern coast—

if you can look past the modern development that has heavily impacted them. Extensive shell middens—represented by broken oyster and clam shells bleached white from centuries of surface exposure to the sun—intermittently line the broad shallow sounds and bays along the outer coastal plain. These trash heaps represent the remains of marine foods that were a dietary mainstay of the coastal Algonkians. Algonkian-speaking groups inhabited the tidewater area of the eastern North American coast at the time of the Europeans' arrival. Our state marks the southern extension of Algonkian settlement that appears to cease just south of the Neuse River around Onslow County. Archaeologically, the material traits that we find associated with Algonkian-related sites include shell-tempered pottery, longhouse structures, and ossuaries, or mass graves.

ECU recently performed one of the most extensive excavations of a coastal Late Woodland site at Hammocks Beach State Park in Onslow County. While Bear Island is the park's main attraction, the area also includes a visitors' center and associated facilities that cover several acres. During the fall of 1997, in agreement with the North Carolina Division of Parks and Recreation and the Office of State Archaeology, I directed archaeological investigations at the west end of the park mainland. Our excavations were done in anticipation of the construction of a new visitors' center that

East Carolina University excavations at Hammocks Beach State Park: storage pit excavation (foreground); cooking pit excavation (background).
(Image originally appeared in *1999 Archaeological Excavations at Hammocks Beach West (31ON665): A Woodland Shell-Midden on the North Carolina Coast.* Photo by Randy Daniel.)

would severely impact a known Late Woodland site. Our excavations confirmed that significant and relatively undisturbed archaeological remains were buried over much of the six-acre project tract. A suite of radiocarbon dates, obtained from various site contexts, suggests that the primary occupation of the site took place during the fourteenth century. So, while the occupants of this portion of the coast lived some two hundred years before the Raleigh expedition encountered natives further up the North Carolina coast, the archaeological evidence we recovered suggests that the village arrangement and daily activities at the site were not significantly different than those of the historic Algonkians that English explorers encountered in the sixteenth century.

The most obvious characteristic of the site was an extensive but highly disturbed shell midden that bordered most of the shoreline. In fact, the upper level of the site was so disturbed by modern plowing that we used a backhoe to mechanically strip the disturbed remains to facilitate quickly locating undisturbed archaeological deposits. About 3,300 square feet of the site surface, at various locations both within and outside the midden, were excavated in this manner. Consequently, over 200 archaeological "features"—most of which were cooking pits or storage pits—were uncovered and mapped; over fifty of these features were completely or partially hand-excavated. Over 4,600 artifacts were recovered during the excavations. Pottery constituted the vast majority of the recovered artifacts, primarily including shell-tempered and fabric-impressed ware. A few stone and bone tools comprised the remainder of the artifact assemblage.

Features were scattered almost continuously in the midden area, but decreased in occurrence with distance away from the midden. Cooking pits were relatively shallow, small circular pits about 1.5 feet in diameter and eight inches deep. Careful analysis of the pit contents provided much information concerning the daily activities of the site's inhabitants. For instance, it appears that cooking pits contained the remnants of family meals and other household refuse, including fish, shellfish, charcoal, and broken pottery. These pits probably served first to cook food and then, after the meal was eaten, acted as a receptacle for the meal's waste and other domestic refuse. Oyster shell and estuarine fish remains recovered from these pits suggest that marine resources were the dietary mainstays of the site's inhabitants, while deer and rabbit remains suggest that mainland game supplemented their diet. Likewise, charred plant remains like nuts, acorns, grapes, and even corn recovered from these features suggest that both wild and domesticated plant foods balanced the coastal diet. Perhaps these early settlers enjoyed a form of hush puppies with their oysters and fish, as do coastal residents today.

Storage pits were oval to circular in shape and about three feet wide and two feet deep, exhibiting rounded sides and bottoms. While, like cooking pits, they also contained domestic refuse, they are interpreted to have served originally as underground facilities designed to conceal

A Theodore de Bry engraving (1590) of a John White drawing (1585) of the coastal Algonkian village of Pomeiock. While archaeological evidence for structures from the coast is consistent with a longhouse design, some potential discrepancies exist between the construction practices illustrated in the White and de Bry depictions and those seen archaeologically. For example, the vertical support poles forming the longhouse frames in this illustration appear to be several feet apart. In contrast, archaeological evidence along the North Carolina coast indicates construction intervals of no more than one foot apart—and more often spaced only a few inches apart. Similarly, archaeological evidence from the coast suggests that support poles were no more than two to four inches in diameter; more substantial posts are indicated in the drawings. These discrepancies remain unresolved.
(courtesy of the North Carolina Collection, University of North Carolina Library at Chapel Hill)

personal items such as pots, fishing gear, and stone tools. This gear was not needed when the site was seasonally abandoned and its inhabitants pursued different subsistence activities farther inland.

Careful excavation also revealed the apparent remains of most of one structure, recognized by a pattern of small circular "postmold" stains in the subsoil characteristic of a longhouse. It measured about fifty-four feet long by fourteen feet wide. Presumably, this longhouse appeared like those Algonkian longhouses depicted in John White's sixteenth-century drawings, which were later engraved by Theodore de Bry. Longhouse walls were constructed of a single row of vertical poles set in the ground and lashed together with horizontal supports, creating a barrel-vaulted framework. Woven reed mats or tree boughs covered the building frame. Such construction is seen as an adaptation to the coastal climate.

Taken together, the artifacts, features, plant, and animal remains suggest that Hammocks Beach West probably was occupied by families who exploited the sound's resources for some portion of the warm season—and possibly longer. Nevertheless, the site's occupants found it necessary to leave at some point during their stay, and in so doing, cached gear they would not need in their move elsewhere. The site was revisited, however, and large deposits of shell eventually accumulated along the shoreline. I should emphasize that my interpretation of a temporary seasonal occupation at Hammocks Beach West contrasts with current views of Late Woodland settlement that stress more sedentary coastal habitations.

The Algonkians are also known for a distinctive type of burial practice whereby large numbers of individuals are buried in a mass grave, or ossuary. Although we did not encounter any such feature at Hammocks Beach, it is likely that one remains nearby. David Phelps has excavated several ossuaries in Currituck County and Carteret County, and on Hatteras Island. They contained between forty and sixty individuals of both sexes ranging from newborn to old age. Prior to burial, the dead were stored in a burial facility referred to as a charnel house. Charnel houses were widespread in the Southeast during historic times.

A Theodore de Bry engraving (1590) of a John White drawing (1585) of a coastal Algonkian charnel house.
(courtesy of the North Carolina Collection, University of North Carolina Library at Chapel Hill)

They were designed to shelter the dead when they reached various stages of decomposition. Such a facility is depicted in one of John White's watercolors. It consists of a simple platform structure that is covered and walled; several corpses line the platform floor. At some point the remains were removed from the charnel houses and placed in an ossuary pit. Skeletal remains unearthed in these pits indicate the deceased were in various stages of decomposition, depending upon their length of stay in the charnel house. For instance, some ossuaries included incomplete bundles of disarticulated bones that suggest a lengthy stay in the charnel house, yet other remains were fully articulated when deposited. Few artifacts accompany the remains.

Contact Period (after ca. A.D. 1550)

Another Algonkian site near Buxton on Hatteras Island has received intermittent archaeological excavation by David Phelps over the last several years. This site is thought to be Croatan, the capital of the Croatan chiefdom among the Algonkians. It was initially tested in 1983 and the present excavations began in 1993. This site has received considerable public attention amid the speculation that it is related to the famous "Lost Colony." Excavations have focused on a midden area of the site, uncovering firepits, pottery, and animal bone. Of particular interest are European trade artifacts, including two copper farthings dating from no earlier than the 1670s. Both have tiny holes drilled in them, possibly indicating that they were worn as jewelry. While most of the European artifacts recovered thus far would have been manufactured too late to be associated with early English settlement attempts, one unique artifact appears to be a material link between the sixteenth-century English settlements and Native Americans. A gold signet ring was discovered during the excavations in 1998. The ring's face exhibits the profile of a prancing lion that probably would have functioned as a family crest to create an impression on wax seals. The crest is distinctive enough that researchers at the College of Arms in London have tentatively identified it as belonging to the Kendall family. Interestingly, two men with the surname Kendall were part of the Roanoke colonization efforts in the 1580s. It remains to be seen if either of these two men can be positively identified as the ring's owner.

In any event, the ring appears to have been modified prior to being lost or discarded. The ring's band is cut or broken and then curled in such a way as to close the gap. This modification has led to the speculation that it was attached to a cord so that it might have been worn on a necklace. The recovery and condition of the ring raise many questions. How did the ring come to be located at the Croatan site? Was the ring lost or traded by either Kendall? Would an Algonkian have modified the ring for use on a necklace rather than a finger? What, if anything, does the ring tell us about the fate of the English colonists? More to the point, what should archaeological evidence of the Lost Colony look like? We may never know the fate of these early settlers, but the discovery of artifacts like this gold ring does fuel the imagination regarding the nature of personal encounters between New World and Old World individuals.

Largely contemporaneous with the Algonkian groups of the Tidewater coast were the neighboring Tuscarora, whose territory covered the inner coastal plain of the northeastern part of the state. Again, much of what we know about the early- and contact-period Tuscarora comes from long-term survey and excavation programs by ECU archaeologists. Because this work is still being analyzed, only preliminary results are available. To date, John Byrd has reported on Tuscarora foodways and settlement practices. The distribution of historic Tuscarora communities has been particularly well-documented by Byrd's archaeological survey of the Contentnea Creek drainage in Greene County. Tuscarora settlement practices included small villages and home-steads located along the major rivers, often near the confluence of a river and small stream. In particular, settlements were located on prime agricultural plots along rivers. This settlement con-figuration is interpreted to represent a strategy whereby villages were positioned near fertile agricultural lands, while also being near reliable and abundant aquatic resources. Domestic crops include an emphasis on corn and beans and possibly other cultigens as well. Non-native crops such as peaches—undoubtedly introduced by European contact—apparently were also a com-mon part of Tuscarora diet by the turn of the eighteenth century.

Most of what we know about the early Tuscarora comes from one site excavated by David Phelps along the Roanoke River in Bertie County. Although no house patterns were uncovered, several pit features, hearths, and burials were found. A portion of the remains of a palisade or stockade that would have surrounded the village, covering about three acres, was also identified. Defining early Tuscarora ceramic types and food practices has been a focus of this site research. Tuscarora pottery was tempered with small pebbles, in contrast to the crushed oyster shells used to temper Algonkian pottery. In some instances, this temper is particularly apparent as pebbles project through the vessel walls. One completed study by John Byrd concerning early Tuscarora food practices indicates that the animal and plant remains recovered at the site suggest a mixed diet based on agriculture, hunting, gathering, and fishing. The river appears to have been an important food source, providing an abundance of fish, freshwater mussels, and turtles. The diversity and abundance of food was such that some early-period villages were never entirely abandoned; at least some occupants inhabited these villages year-round. Such sedentism, how-ever, was altered by participation in the European deerskin trade. As written accounts document, the historic-period Tuscarora are also known to have partially abandoned their villages in the winter, establishing temporary camps to hunt deer. Archaeologists are uncertain about how common this practice was prior to native participation in the European deerskin trade.

We also have some limited evidence concerning burial practices that, along with written accounts of the period, suggest that status differences were present among the Tuscarora. As is the case with Algonkian burial practices, early Tuscarora burial sites are usually ossuaries, as they contain more than one individual deposited as secondary bundle burials. Still, an important distinction can be made between Tuscarora and Algonkian ossuaries in that the smaller number of individuals in the former is interpreted to represent a family unit, rather than the multi-family community burials represented by the larger ossuaries of the latter. Marginella shell beads—some recovered as if deposited strung together—are a common artifact associated with burials. The beads occur in varying quantities that may have indicated social status or rank; we are not yet certain of this pattern. Written accounts of early European settlers in the region, however, do suggest that sociopolitical distinctions did exist among the Tuscarora. For instance, when Christoph von Graffenried, the founder of New Bern and leader of Swiss and German settlers in the area, contacted the Tuscarora in the eighteenth century, he noted the presence of "chiefs" and "kings" among village leaders and that this leadership was hereditary. Apparently, at least by this point in time, the Tuscarora distinguished some form of ascribed status within its villages, perhaps even distinguishing ranks among its leaders.

The Tuscarora site in the region that has received the most archaeological attention is not typical of traditional settlement practices. Neoheroka Fort in Greene County has been excavated virtually every summer for the last ten years. The results of this work have not yet been reported, but some preliminary statements can be made. Neoheroka Fort was one of at least a dozen forts built by natives during the Contact Period to protect groups living in dispersed villages. In 1713, Neoheroka was the site of the last major battle of the Tuscarora War. This battle marked the end of a three-year war between North Carolina colonists and some Tuscarora villages. The war was a result of frustrations experienced by the Tuscarora over years of land-grabbing, slave raiding, dishonest trading practices, and epidemic diseases. On the morning of September 22, 1711, this frustration culminated in an Indian attack on colonists living along the Neuse and Pamlico rivers. Ironically, rather than continuing their traditional battle tactics in the form of ambush or early-morning surprise attacks, the Tuscarora decided to defend themselves in a fort modeled after a European design. Arguably, this tactic sealed their fate—or at least hastened it. In any event, excavations have uncovered most of the fort outline, including several bastions. The fort covered over an acre and housed native men, women, and children. Excavations in the fort interior have also revealed several dozen pithouse-like structures that were interconnected by a series of tunnels. Presumably, family groups occupied each structure.

In mid-March 1713, after a three-day siege, the fort was put to the torch by a contingent of white soldiers and Indian mercenaries. The burning resulted in almost Pompeii-like site preservation, providing a snapshot of a scene that took place almost 300 years ago. Household goods, including pottery, stone tools, and other domestic items, were found lying on the structure's floors. Abundant food supplies were uncovered in storage areas of the houses, including the remains of corn, beans, and even peaches.

An estimated 1,000 Tuscarora were either killed or captured, or fled the area as a result of this battle. Consequently, the Tuscarora were greatly reduced in number and lost most of their land. Throughout the latter part of the eighteenth century, many of the remaining groups moved north to join the Iroquois. Likewise, encounters between native Algonkians and other Europeans resulted in disastrous effects. By the dawn of the eighteenth century, Old World diseases and colonial expansion into native territories had reduced by half the number of coastal Algonkians in North Carolina. Within the next few decades, Algonkian cultures in the area completely dissipated.

Conclusion

In just three decades of research, East Carolina University has contributed much to our knowledge about coastal plain prehistory. I have highlighted a few of those contributions here, selecting those which have been (or might become) prominent in their impact on our discipline. Much work, however, remains to be done. As the reader may have noted from this essay, we know considerably less about the early time periods of the region than we do about later ones. Similarly, much less is known about the southern coastal plain than about the northern half. Nevertheless, if the next thirty years prove as productive as the first thirty, I am confident we will have made significant strides toward understanding the ancient cultures of eastern North Carolina.

RECOMMENDATIONS FOR FURTHER READING

Byrd, John E. *Tuscarora Subsistence Patterns in the Late Woodland Period: The Zooarchaeology of the Jordan's Landing Site.* Raleigh, NC: North Carolina Archaeological Council Pub. No. 27, 1977.

Daniel, I. Randolph, Jr. "Stone Raw Material and Early Archaic Settlement in the Southeastern United States." *American Antiquity* 66 (2001): 237–265.

_____. "North Carolina Paleoindian Points." *Current Research in the Pleistocene* 17 (2000): 14–16.

_____. "Archaeological Excavations at Hammocks Beach West (31ON665): A Woodland Shell-midden on the North Carolina Coast." *Occasional Papers of the Phelps Archaeology Laboratory*, No. 1, Greenville, NC: Department of Anthropology & Phelps Archaeology Laboratory, East Carolina University, 1999.

Herbert, Joseph M. (compiler). "Prehistoric Pottery: Series and Sequence on the Carolina Coast." *North Carolina Archaeology* 48 (1999).

Phelps, David S. "Archaeology of the North Carolina Coast and Coastal Plain: Problems and Hypotheses." In *Prehistory of North Carolina: An Archaeological Symposium.* M.A. Mathis and J.A. Crow, eds. Raleigh, NC: North Carolina Division of Archives and History, 1983.

Shields, E. Thomson, Jr. "Family Crest on Sixteenth-Century Gold Ring Tentatively Identified." *Roanoke Colonies Research Newsletter* 6 (1999): 2.

Ward, H. Trawick and R.P. Stephen Davis, Jr. *Time Before History: The Archaeology of North Carolina.* Chapel Hill, NC: UNC Press, 1996.

Boat Building the Harkers Island Way

— Carmine Prioli —

"The length, the width, the depth, all of that, it's in your mind. You make your keel and you cut your frame and you go to puttin' together and puttin' together, until you got 'er finished, and she comes out a nice-looking boat."

—James Rose, Harkers Island boat builder, quoted in *Coastwatch* (1980)

*L*ongtime residents of Harkers Island believe that boat building is a skill that is embedded in their genes. Take what islanders affectionately call a "youngern" off the island at birth and raise him far inland. Raleigh, for example, or some other place distant from the ocean. When he's about sixteen, turn him loose in a workshop with pine and juniper. Without plans or instructions of any sort, he'll automatically assemble something with a flared bow, a wide beam, and a 4:1 sheer, just like the rugged work boats that for generations have plowed the waters and kicked the Down East mud of Bogue and Back and Core sounds.

Folk beliefs aside, boat building is an unremarkable activity for most island boys, who in their early grade-school years begin fashioning toy boats with scrap lumber. With help from a father or older brother, construction of a fourteen-foot skiff might occur at around age ten. The process is as natural to island youth as assembling soapbox racers and tree houses is to their mainland counterparts. But on Harkers Island adolescent boat building is not just play. It is a form of initiation into a culture attuned as much to moving on water as to riding on dry land.

During the first decades of the present century, the demand for Harkers Island-built boats was confined to the Down East region. While boats constructed on the island continued to be made by traditional methods, the innovations devised by Brady Lewis (1904–1992) eventually led to a demand for Harkers Island boats that went far beyond the island itself. Originally from Salter Path, Lewis was probably a descendant of the Lewises who emigrated from Shackleford Banks in the 1890s. In the early 1930s, he moved to Harkers Island with his wife and father to build and repair work boats.

Lewis became locally renowned as the man who gave the sturdy Harkers Island workboat a feature known as the "flare" or "flowered" bow, for the way its inward curves resemble flower

The "flare" bow at work in the Gulf Stream. (photo by Carmine Prioli)

petals in full bloom. In addition to the esthetic appeal of the bow's graceful upward sweep, the feature was intended to deflect water in choppy seas.

The uninitiated viewer, accustomed to seeing the often-exaggerated flare of modern fiberglass hulls, might wonder about the significance of Lewis's accomplishment. It is a relatively simple process to mold fiberglass to a curved form. But in the days before man-made materials, adapting wood to graceful curves without the use of steam demanded unusual skill and imagination.

Along with the islanders' reputation for building strong, maneuverable boats, the flare bow design became a Harkers Island trademark that attracted the attention—and the dollars—of non-island commercial and sport fishermen from New England to Florida. For nearly a quarter-century now, large manufacturers of expensive sport fishing craft have imitated the flare by molding it into their mass-produced "plastic" hulls.

Despite the popularity of the flare bow among sport fishermen, local watermen have mixed feelings about the feature that made their boat building tradition famous and, at one time, prosperous. When commercial fishermen today order a vessel from one of the handful of surviving Harkers Island builders, they might request a boat with only a slight flare. For one thing, there's more labor involved in producing an accentuated inward curve and that feature makes construction more expensive. Fishermen also complain that the concave bow allows less room inside the boat than would normally be provided by the wider expanse of forward deck space. Moreover, the basic structure of the boat is weakened in comparison to a conventional design, because fashioning the proper curve in the rib boards requires cutting into the wood grain. This results in a type of rib that is not as strong as one made from a parallel cut. The difference in strength can be crucial when attempting to tie up at a pier in a driving southwest wind, with a ton or more of freshly caught fish or shellfish on board.

Finally, the accentuated flare's ability to deflect oncoming seas is also a matter of some debate. Many of the commercial fishermen claim that, under the right conditions, a sheet of water will actually be trapped in the flare, only to be blown into the boat when it climbs upward. So why does this feature continue to be popular among recreational boat buyers? Shortly before his death Brady Lewis was asked why he developed the flare bow, and he responded simply by saying, "They're pretty."[1] Peter Willis, a former Harkers Island boat builder, agrees. "It is nice-looking," he says, but "it's more *looks* than anything else."[2]

At least as important as the flare bow design he popularized was the influence Brady Lewis had in helping to spawn the commercial boat building industry on Harkers Island. Until the hurricanes of the mid-1950s destroyed his boat works, Lewis was the master of commercial boat construction. Several of the island's major boat builders—including James T. Gillikin, James and Earl L. Rose, Julian Guthrie, and Clem Willis—worked for Lewis before they established their own businesses.

At one time, there were forty-two active boat builders on the island. Although most of them alternated boat construction with working the water, more than a dozen builders managed to make a living primarily by assembling wooden boats using a combination of traditional and modern materials. The largest and one of the most luxurious of all the vessels produced on the island was the seventy-four-foot pleasure yacht, *Atlas*. Launched from the Rose Brothers Boat Works in February 1970 at a cost of around $250,000, the boat had sleeping facilities for twelve

The forty-foot fishing vessel Jean & Dale *is the only known boat built by Brady Lewis still in existence on Harkers Island. She was constructed in 1941 at a cost of $750, which at the time made her the most expensive boat built on the island. In 2000, after the death of Harry M. Lewis (for nearly sixty years the boat's only owner), the* Jean & Dale *was donated to the Core Sound Waterfowl Museum. Plans are now underway to restore the vessel and display her as part of the museum's permanent collection.*
(photo by Carmine Prioli)

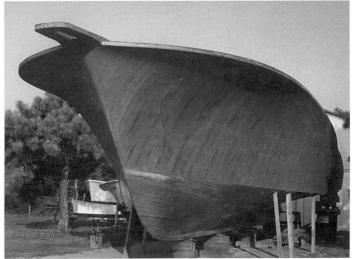

(ABOVE) *A work boat under construction the hand-crafted way. Jamie Lewis, master boatwright, is shown here trimming the stem of a work boat with a ship carpenter's adze, locally known as an "edge." Such ancient boat building practices and hand tools are still common among the few full-time builders on the island.* (photo by Carmine Prioli)

(ABOVE RIGHT) *This nearly-complete wooden hull shows the furniture-like quality that is usually concealed beneath the surface paint of Harkers Island sport fishing vessels. Lewis Brothers Boat Works, Harkers Island.* (photo by Carmine Prioli)

and was outfitted with central heating and air conditioning, bars, stereos, color television, and automatic pilot.[3]

The *Atlas* was one of scores of large pleasure and commercial craft produced during the heyday of Harkers Island boat building. The twenty-year period from the mid-fifties to the mid-seventies was the most prosperous one for the islanders, with the Rose Brothers Boat Works alone floating fourteen boats in the forty-foot range or longer from 1973 to 1976.[4] But the boom was not to last. By 1979 changes that originated far beyond Carteret County were affecting the island's economy, changes that not even the appeal of wood and the aroma of juniper could stave off.

"You'll still find a boat in nearly every yard," reported *Coastwatch* in May 1979, "but commercial fishermen and boat builders make up a dwindling portion of the population."[5] The disappearance of maritime forests throughout the coastal region made lumber more expensive, but this was not the only factor. The high cost of labor and a diminishing labor pool, the energy crisis of the 1970s, and the double-digit interest rates of the 1980s all adversely affected the island's chief manufacturing industry.

Finally, throughout the 1970s the demand for fiberglass boats greatly reduced the market for wooden boats. Although fiberglass vessels are more expensive to purchase than wooden boats, the extra cost is quickly offset by much lower maintenance expenses and higher resale value. Especially in the Southeast, where environmental conditions (heat, dampness, and wood-boring worms) are especially hard on wooden boats, fiberglass quickly outstripped wood as the preferred material.

Yet among many islanders and a small number of enthusiasts, the appeal of wood remains irresistible.[6] There is even a theory among some offshore sport fishermen that the unique vibrations emitted by wooden hulls attract big game fish to the surface and, in turn, to the lures trailing behind the boat. And according to Peter Willis, a wooden boat will serve its owner just as faithfully as fiberglass. If properly cared for, it could last a lifetime. "You know," Peter remarked, "there's probably some [boats] around that are *fifty* years old. A guy use one fifty years, he don't need her any longer!"[7]

Now only three full-time boat building operations exist on Harkers Island. They survive by adjusting traditional skills to the realities of today's marketplace. Lewis Brothers Boat Works, Alex Willis Boat Construction, Inc., and East Bay Boat Works still specialize in the wooden designs that have become Harkers Island trademarks, but their boats usually display a glossy skin of fiberglass, protecting the juniper strips that lie beneath it.

East Bay Boat Works has gone a step further than the others. While it continues to produce boats of the traditional Harkers Island design, it is also turning out wooden sport fishing craft structurally unlike anything the island has seen, and to most eyes virtually indistinguishable from their mass-produced fiberglass

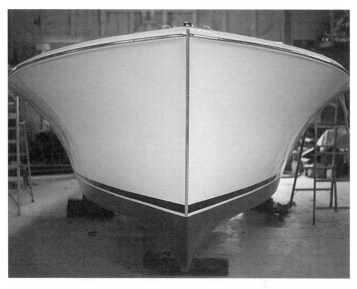

(ABOVE) *An upscale version of an open-hulled skiff showing the distinctive Harkers Island "flare." With a glossy coat of fiberglass protecting its juniper planking, this vessel is designed more for pleasure boating than for working the sounds. Lewis Brothers Boat Works, Harkers Island.* (photo by Carmine Prioli)

(BELOW) *A "play" boat under construction, using the "tortured" plywood technique. This method of construction enables the creation of curves and compound bends that would have challenged the abilities of even the early master boat builders. East Boat Bay Works, Harkers Island.* (photo by Carmine Prioli)

counterparts. There, a younger generation of builders led by Ricky Gillikin turn out "play" boats in the thirty- to forty-foot range, by what is known locally as the "tortured plywood" method. Extremely light-framed and thin-skinned, these boats are intended for use as pleasure craft and they are built for speed. Space-age epoxy cement and a process known as "cold-molding" allow the shaping of plywood into compound bends. The results are seagoing vessels whose structural integrity rivals the heavier pine-framed boats and accentuated flares that even Brady Lewis may never have imagined possible.

Gillikin's boats are sleek, fast, and, like their traditional predecessors, they are essentially wood-built. As such, they exemplify a genius for adaptation. And they are enabling some islanders to continue an ancestral way of life that has endured for nearly a hundred years.

ENDNOTES

1. Brian Blomquist, "Journey in Search of Living Legend Ends," *Carteret County News-Times*, February 29, 1988.

2. Interview, March 17, 1994.

3. Jim Linn, "Everything's Ship Shape," *The News and Observer* (Raleigh), May 27, 1973.

4. Phil Bowie, "Harkers Island Boats," *Motorboat* (January 1976), 89.

5. "Of Corncob Pipes and Mullet Fishing," *Coastwatch* (May 1979), n.p. See also Ann Green, "Shipshape: Harkers Island Boatbuilders Keep Tradition Alive," *Coastwatch* (Winter 1999): 14–18.

6. For an account of the appeal of wooden boats, see Louis Rubin, *Small Craft Advisory: The Building of a Wooden Boat* (Boston: Atlantic Monthly Press, 1993).

7. Interview, March 17, 1994.

African Americans by the Sea

— Walt Wolfram —

*A*lthough it may not be apparent to the casual visitor, African Americans have played an important role in the development of the waterways of coastal North Carolina. Only recently, in works like David S. Cecelski's *The Waterman's Song: Slavery and Freedom in Maritime North Carolina* (2001) have historians begun to tell their story.

Much like the prehistoric Native American populations of the past and the emerging Hispanic populations of the future, African Americans by the sea have often been invisible, despite the fact that, between 1800 and 1860, they comprised almost fifty percent of the total population of the sixteen tidewater counties. The coastal region has never been an exclusive ethnic enclave, and there are some longstanding African-American communities and families that have been and continue to be a significant part of the coastal tradition. They have fished the waters of the sea and sounds, piloted ships around the dangerous shoals and through the narrow channels of the waterways, harvested the crops from the fertile soils, and safeguarded the coast for hundreds of years.

Most of the first African Americans in the region were brought there as slaves from Virginia and Maryland, starting in the early 1700s. By the mid-1700s, records indicate that African Americans made up a quarter to a third of the overall population of coastal North Carolina. Up through the Civil War, even the Outer Banks islands had significant slave populations. Ocracoke had a population that included over a hundred slaves at the time of the Civil War, and mainland Hyde County near the Pamlico Sound had a single plantation with over two hundred slaves.

Many African-American slaves became skilled watermen, and were heavily involved in fishing, ferrying, and piloting; their expertise quickly became essential to the maritime culture and economy of coastal North Carolina. At the same time, recent studies have indicated a strong undercurrent to their life on the water, including what David Cecelski calls a "maritime section of the Underground Railroad" that flourished along North Carolina's coastal waterways for more than sixty years. The combination of skillful African-American watermen and a conspiring network of freedmen, fugitive slaves, and sailors situated within the complex geography of rivers, estuaries, pocosins, and tidal marshes along the coast offered an opportunistic landscape for a maritime route to freedom. By the mid-1800s, this coastal escape route had become such a common passageway to freedom that one Wilmington correspondent lamented that it was "an everyday occurrence for negro slaves to take passage [aboard a ship] and go North" (Cecelski, "The Shores of Freedom," 174).

Although the Civil War changed the lives of many African Americans on the Outer Banks and altered the demographics of particular coastal locations, the ratio of African Americans to whites in the overall coastal population did not change appreciably. For example, the slave populations of island communities such as Hatteras, Portsmouth, Ocracoke, and Harkers Island were largely depleted during this time, but Roanoke Island became a large enclave for ex-slaves and the site of a freedmen's colony.

During the Civil War, the Union army considered it essential to control the coastal waterways, so in 1862 over 11,000 Union troops overwhelmed and defeated the Confederate forces on Roanoke Island. Following their occupation, and in honor of General Ambrose Burnside who led the Union attack on the Island, the Union army built Fort Burnside on the north end of the island. The federal government then established an official Freedmen's Colony as a refugee camp for freed and escaped slaves. The plan for the island, as outlined in one of the early charges, was to "establish a colony of negroes upon Roanoke Island...to settle colored people on the unoccupied lands, and to give them agricultural and mechanical tools to begin with, and to train and educate them for a free and independent community" (Stick 162). Within a few years, this village grew to more than 600 houses, and included a sawmill, a school, a hospital, a church, and a store. By 1865, there were over 3,000 African-American refugees in the colony. However, an order to restore the land to the original owners was issued in 1866, ending the experimental community and scattering the residents.

Farther down the coast at Beaufort, a couple of hundred African Americans received assistance during the Union occupation there, but many African Americans continued to work on the water. Their work included oystering, fishing, and boating. For example, over a hundred African-American men were involved in operating small passenger and freight boats between Morehead City and Beaufort, extending services to Fort Macon, Shackleford Banks, and other locations during this period.

In 1863, when it became possible for African Americans to enlist in the Union army, within a brief period over a hundred men from the coast joined, and became part of the Thirty-Sixth United States Colored Troop. These troops participated in Union operations ranging from South Carolina to Maryland, including an important victory over Robert E. Lee's troops in New Market, Virginia, that led to the defeat of the Confederate capital in Richmond, Virginia. During the battle, twenty-six men were killed, eighty-seven were wounded, and two received Congressional Medals of Honor for bravery. Some of the men who served in this infantry troop returned to contribute in significant ways to life on the North Carolina coast.

African Americans not only worked on the water; they helped rescue people from its fury, and, during times of war, also protected the coastline from potential invaders. One of the distinguished traditions of the Outer Banks was the U.S. Lifesaving Service, established in 1871 to help rescue the victims of shipwrecks along the treacherous coast of the Atlantic Ocean. A lifesaving station typically consisted of a "keeper" in charge of the operation and six surfmen who were responsible for rescues. These crews were typically staffed by whites, with an occasional African American employed at the lowest rank, Surfman No. 6. In 1879, however, the inspector in charge of Pea Island boldly fired several incompetent white crew members and replaced the keeper with Richard Etheridge, a surfman at the Oregon Inland station who had served with the Thirty-Sixth Colored Troop and had been an active member of the Roanoke Freedmen's Colony. In his appointment, he was described as "as good a surfman as there is on the coast, black or white" (Weatherford 38). The remaining white surfmen at the station resigned in protest and were replaced by African Americans, thus forming the first exclusively black lifesaving station on the Outer Banks. Despite the burning of the station after the first season of operation, the crew endured and the station became a model, all-black lifesaving station—until the Coast Guard finally closed it in 1947. Although the crew was involved in a number of rescue efforts, including a heroic effort in which they saved nine people on the schooner *E.S. Newman* in the midst of a hurricane in 1896, their achievements went largely unrecognized. Finally, a century later, the Pea Island lifesavers posthumously received the Gold Lifesaving Medal for their heroic action.

Today, there are various small African-American communities dotting the coastal mainland that have participated in the ways of the water, but on the Outer Banks islands, each island seems to be represented only by a single long-term family. For example, in the twentieth century, Ocracoke, Hatteras, Hog Island, Cedar Island, and Portsmouth Island have all had only one permanent black family on their respective islands. In most cases, the family simply stayed on the island when freed slaves left the islands en masse after the Civil War. In one instance, however, a single African-American family moved to the Outer Banks following the war. Each of these respective families fashioned their own identities in relation to the surrounding white community, but there are parallels in their social relations. For example, there was a level of acceptance that included African Americans in many community activities, with virtually no reported acts of overt hostility toward them. At the same time, there was also a complicit under- standing of differential social roles for African Americans reflected in the existence of statewide Jim Crow laws barring blacks from attending the white schools during segregation and prohibit- ing marriage to whites.

Each of the isolated African-American families on the Outer Banks has a special story. One such story involves the Bryant family of Ocracoke. In the 1860s, as the slave population of Ocracoke dispersed after the Civil War, a former slave family from Blount's Creek, located near Washington, North Carolina, took a steamboat to Ocracoke and settled there. Harkus (Hercules) Blount was a boat builder and carpenter and his wife, Winnie Blount, was a domestic and picked clams from their shells at the Doxee Clam Factory in Ocracoke. They had two children, one of whom, Acey Jane, stayed on the island. There she met her husband, Leonard Bryant, who was originally from Engelhard, North Carolina, but was living in New Bern. He came to the island to work for the Doxees, loading and unloading the boats that carried the clams. Leonard Bryant and Acey Jane Blount fell in love, married, and had nine living children, five boys and four girls.

Most of the Bryant children left the island, but several of them stayed and became part of the island community. For example, one son, Julius, participated in many of the typical activities for Ocracoke men, fishing, playing poker, and drinking homemade meal wine while strumming his guitar and singing the traditional island songs. He is remembered fondly by the islanders, but he could not attend the legally segregated school nor marry an island woman. He learned to read, as did his brothers and sisters, from volunteer teachers after school hours, and did not marry until he finally moved to mainland Hyde County near the end of his life. At the writing of this article, only Muzel Bryant, born in 1904, remains of the Bryant family on Ocracoke. She

is a gracious woman, with a remarkable aptitude for recounting historical stories and dates. At age ninety-six, she could recall all of the birth dates of her siblings and could recount many details of past events that have faded from the memories of other islanders. She now passes the time reading and watching TV in the island home of Ken Ballance, while remaining a most hospitable host to those who drop by to say hello or share some food. She is an island treasure, largely unseen by outsiders but well known and greatly appreciated by those who have known her all their lives. When she is gone, there will be no one to carry on her name in Ocracoke.

Muzel Bryant, last surviving descendant of Ocracoke's only African-American family (1999). (photos by Scott Taylor)

Perhaps symbolically, the most newsworthy event about the Bryant family involved their oldest son, Artis, who was born on Ocracoke in 1902. He left the island for Philadelphia in 1916 to work on the dredges and rarely, if ever, returned. During World War II, he served on an all-black crew of a merchant marine ship that was torpedoed by German U2 boats in the Atlantic Ocean near the coast. The boat carrying the survivors beached at the closest land site, which turned out to be his homeland island of Ocracoke. According to the reports of his sisters, who were there at the time, he left the next day and never again returned. Newspaper accounts from that time verify Artis Bryant's fortuitous return to Ocracoke, but they could not testify to the loneliness felt by his siblings and parents as an isolated African-American family that lost its members to the mainland. As the islands expand to include tourists from all over the United States and the world, the presence of African Americans on the Outer Banks continues to fade. Those who truly know the islands, though, surely remember the indelible imprint of the African-American presence there.

BIBLIOGRAPHIC NOTES

For a general account of African Americans on the Outer Banks, see David Stick, *The Outer Banks of North Carolina, 1584–1958* (Chapel Hill/London: UNC Press, 1956, pp. 161–167). A more specific account of coastal African Americans is David Cecelski's thoroughly researched essay, "The Shores of Freedom: The Maritime Underground Railroad in North Carolina, 1800–1861," in *The North Carolina Historical Review*, LXXI:2 (April 1994): 174–206. See also Cecelski's more recent book, *The Waterman's Song: Slavery and Freedom in Maritime North Carolina* (Chapel Hill/London: UNC Press, 2001). The population demographics of the early coastal region can be found in Marvin L. Michael Kay and Lorin Lee Cary, *Slavery in North Carolina, 1748–1775* (Chapel Hill/London: UNC Press, 1995), whereas a description of the Pea Island lifesavers and the life of Richard Etheridge can be found in Carole Boston Weatherford, *Sink or Swim: African-American Lifesavers of the Outer Banks* (Wilmington, NC: Coastal Carolina Press, 1999). See Alton Balance's book *Ocracokers*, Chapter 6 (Chapel Hill/London: UNC Press, 1989) for more information on the Bryant family. Walt Wolfram, Kirk Hazen, and Jennifer Ruff Tamburro's article, "Isolation within Isolation: A Solitary Century of African-American Vernacular English," *Journal of Sociolinguistics* 1 (1997): 7–38 gives a technical account of how Muzel Bryant's speech aligns with those of other Ocracokers. See also Walt Wolfram and Erik Thomas, *The Development of African-American English* (Malden/Oxford: Basil Blackwell, 2002). Ellen Fulcher Cloud's *Portsmouth the Way It Was* (Atlantic, NC: Live Oak Publications, 1996) gives an account of a single African-American family on the island of Portsmouth not unlike that of the Bryant family on Ocracoke.

Acknowledgment: The author is greatly indebted to Ellen Fulcher Cloud of Ocracoke for her assistance in the preparation of this article and for her invaluable research on the genealogies of African Americans on the Outer Banks islands of Ocracoke and Portsmouth.

Cape Lookout National Seashore Chronology

1937   Cape Hatteras National Seashore established to include 70 miles of shoreline from Bodie Island to Ocracoke Island.

1938   U.S. Interior Secretary Ickes publicly addresses the question of restricted access to America's beaches.

1959   State of N.C. passes legislation to establish an Outer Banks state park and to stabilize Barden's Inlet.

1962   Ash Wednesday storm demonstrates huge cost of stabilizing and developing barrier islands for public use.

N.C. Seashore Park Commission requests transfer of state-owned Outer Banks property to National Park Service for Cape Lookout National Seashore.

1963   87th Congress: Senate and House bills introduced to establish National Seashore park at Cape Lookout. Core Banks Gun Club land is excluded.

Assassination of President Kennedy postpones all work of 87th Congress.

1964   Bills still under consideration. Governor Sanford states that "almost" all of the land has been acquired.

1965   S. 251 (Senate Bill) receives hearing on the establishment of Cape Lookout Seashore in N.C.:

- 20,000 acres of land
- 10,000 acres of open water
- 58 miles of ocean shoreline

J.M. Davis, Morehead City businessman, demands the same treatment for his "gun club" land as Core Banks Gun Club received.

A. Clark Stratton, assistant director for National Park Service, questioned about the Core Banks Gun Club exclusion.

Senator Bible, chair for the Congressional subcommittee on parks and recreation, is unsatisfied with the unequal treatment given the Core Banks Gun Club, saying: "I do not think this is the way to create a park."

S. 251 receives Senate approval, July 27, 1965.

1966   H.R. 1784 (House Bill) is introduced recommending the establishment of Cape Lookout National Seashore in N.C.

H.R. 1784 receives a hearing on February 1, and is approved soon thereafter.

President Johnson signs PL 89-366 (Public Law) to establish Cape Lookout National Seashore and says he is "glad to be able to talk about something besides Viet Nam."
- $3,200,000 for park development and land acquisition (includes Shackleford Banks)
- 25-year leases granted to legal owners of acquired land
- State of N.C. continues to acquire land and turn it over to the federal government; 80% of Portsmouth Island and Core Banks purchased. Department of Interior to buy Shackleford Banks
- Core Banks Gun Club and Charles M. Reeves land (near Cape Lookout Lighthouse) not yet acquired

National Park Service cannot administer Cape Lookout National Seashore as "single administrative unit" because excluded property cuts across park service land.

Two public workshops held on park's management and land use plan.

1971   Core Banks Gun Club initiates legal maneuver, further encumbering process of land acquisition.

1974   Federal money for land acquisition increased to $7,903,000.

Reeves and Core Banks Gun Club sell their land to State of N.C. for combined total of $4,500,000 and 25-year lease to use the land. They are prompted to settle by introduction of federal legislation to amend 1966 bill to include their property in the seashore.

N.C. Governor Holshauser transfers 28,000 acres of state-owned Core Banks and Portsmouth Island land to federal government.

1978   Federal government files condemnation proceedings for title to 2,369 acres of Shackleford Banks and 2,000 acres of adjacent marshland. Original ownership of much of the land is in doubt due to:
- deeds improperly recorded
- deeds lost
- landform changes

Public workshops spawn five land-use plans for National Seashore.

1980   Park Superintendent "Mack" Riddel proposes wilderness designation for most of the National Seashore land, which would prohibit use of motor vehicles on park beaches.

Without motor vehicles, surf fishermen cannot quickly track fish or transport equipment.

Surf fishermen dominate four public hearings on National Seashore land use. State officials support public petition for controlled use of private vehicles and designation only of Shackleford Banks as wilderness area.

National Seashore officials allow restricted vehicle access along specified beach corridor of Core Banks. Shackleford Banks to become wilderness area.

1985 Shackleford Banks is added to National Seashore Park. No domesticated animals or "exotic" species allowed, except wild horses. Cottages are to be removed.

National Park Service officially informs public to remove animals, structures, and personal property by midnight December 31, 1985.

Cottages set afire on Shackleford Banks. Cape Lookout National Seashore visitors' center on Harkers Island destroyed by fire, December 30, 1985.

1993 Cape Lookout National Seashore headquarters opens on Harkers Island.

Core Sound Waterfowl Museum (described as "a working-man's museum") is granted 75-year lease for 16 acres of land adjacent to National Seashore headquarters.

1997 Groundbreaking ceremony for the Core Sound Waterfowl Museum, January 25, 1997.

1999 Hurricane Floyd creates massive flooding in eastern N.C., delaying completion of Core Sound Waterfowl Museum, subsequently scheduled for 2002 opening.

The Stormy Birth of Cape Lookout National Seashore

— Carmine Prioli —

In 1938, U.S. Interior Secretary Harold C. Ickes was deeply troubled by the fact that so many of his fellow citizens were being denied access to America's beaches. Speaking eloquently for the creation of seashore reservations, like the one on Cape Hatteras that had been established a year earlier, Ickes said:

> When we look up and down the oceanfronts of America, we find that everywhere they are passing behind the fences of private ownership. The people can no longer get to the ocean. When we have reached the point that a nation of 125 million people cannot set foot upon the thousands of miles of beaches that border the Atlantic and Pacific Oceans, except by permission of those who monopolize the oceanfront, then I say it is the prerogative and duty of the Federal and State Governments to step in and acquire, not a swimming beach here and there, but solid blocks of oceanfront hundreds of miles in length. Call this oceanfront a national park, or a national seashore, or a state park or anything you please—I say the people have right to a fair share of it.[1]

With the presence of Cape Hatteras National Seashore stretching from Bodie Island south to Ocracoke, North Carolina already had some seventy miles of shoreline preserved for the use of American citizens. Although far short of the "hundreds of miles" of oceanfront Secretary Ickes envisioned, it was substantial nonetheless. And it inspired some North Carolina officials to see the possibility of extending the seashore park concept southward another fifty-eight miles, by converting Portsmouth Island, Core Banks, and Shackleford Banks to the public trust.

It would take a few years for the idea to gain sufficient public support, but in 1959 the State of North Carolina approved a resolution to establish an Outer Banks state park, just south of the Cape Hatteras National Seashore. With $600,000 appropriated for studies and real estate acquisition, the State began purchasing land on Core Banks and Portsmouth Island. The 1959 bill also authorized the State to acquire "as much of Shackleford Banks as necessary for the stabilization of Barden's Inlet…" With the devastation wrought by the Ash Wednesday storm

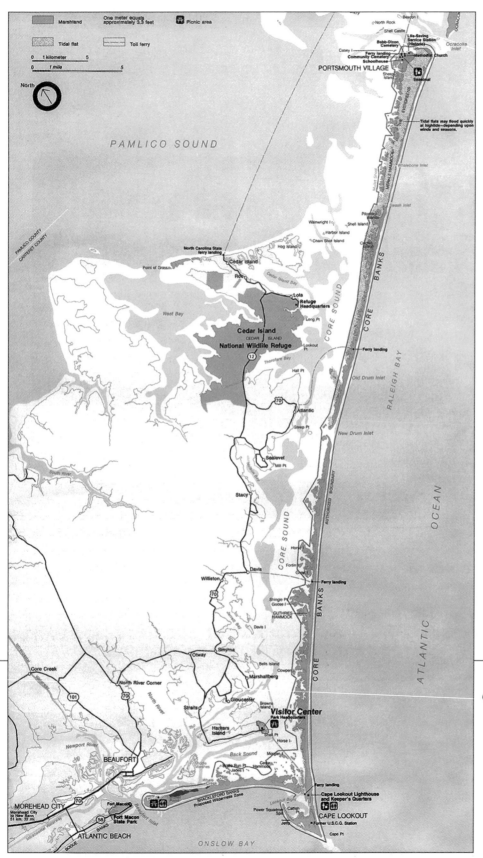

Cape Lookout.

of 1962, however, it became apparent that stabilizing the barrier islands against the forces of nature and developing them for public use would far exceed state resources. The kind of measures believed necessary at the time could only be provided by the federal government, which could assign the Army Corps of Engineers to undertake the project. In an article in *The Washington Post*, Aubrey Graves reported that "Interior Secretary Steward L. Udall suggested the time had come for land adjustment and acquisition by the Federal Government of more ocean-frontages for public purposes, particularly public recreation and wildlife preservation. He huddled with Governor Terry Sanford about the North Carolina seacoast."[2] What Udall had in mind was adding a significant link to the chain of national seashores he imagined running from Cape Cod, Massachusetts, to Padre Island, Texas. The secretary apparently convinced the right people. On September 13, 1963, the North Carolina Seashore Park Commission requested the governor and the council of state to take the necessary steps to transfer state-owned Outer Banks property to the National Park Service for inclusion in a proposed Cape Lookout National Seashore.

North Carolina government officials agreed to acquire the necessary land and donate it to the federal government for park development. By the summer of 1963, government officials were informed that the majority of land negotiations for Portsmouth Island and Core Banks had been finalized. Subsequently, on October 17, 1963, Senators B. Everett Jordan and Sam Ervin introduced Senate Bill 2244, calling for the establishment of a National Seashore park at Cape Lookout to "preserve for public use and enjoyment an area in the State of North Carolina possessing outstanding natural and recreational values..." At the same time, Congressman David N. Henderson introduced an identical bill in the U.S. House of Representatives.

Momentum for the bill's consideration during the 87th Congress apparently was lost with the assassination of President Kennedy in November 1963. On March 13, 1964, with the Cape Lookout National Seashore bill still not under consideration, Governor Terry Sanford wrote to Secretary Udall, saying that North Carolina had acquired "almost" all the property needed for the proposed national seashore and that "the way has been cleared in North Carolina" for congressional approval. "Anything you can do to push this along," Sanford added, "will be appreciated."[3]

Clearly, North Carolina officials were eager to see the federal government's presence extended on their coastline. But contrary to Governor Sanford's assurance, the way had not been cleared sufficiently. By 1964, several thousand acres of land had been purchased for the seashore park, but the owners of at least one parcel were holding out. The eighteen or so members of the Core Sound Gun Club thought their 900 + acre tract on the sound side of Core Banks, about fourteen miles north of Cape Lookout, was worth more than the $20 an acre the State had paid for land adjacent to theirs. Apparently hoping to sidestep the issue at least temporarily, the bill's sponsors excluded the gun club property from the bill. On June 3, 1965, Senator Alan Bible of Nevada, chairman of the subcommittee on parks and recreation, convened a hearing on the legislation which—now designated as S. 251—would "provide for the establishment of the Cape Lookout National Seashore in the State of North Carolina."[4]

Bible announced that the proposed national seashore would embrace approximately 20,000 acres of land and marsh, and another 10,000 acres of open water. Its fifty-eight miles of ocean shoreline would constitute one of the longest stretches of undeveloped ocean beach on the eastern seaboard, extending from Ocracoke Inlet on the north to Beaufort Inlet on the south and west. "We anticipate," Senator Bible noted, "that the State of North Carolina will donate to the

United States all but 2,700 acres of the land within the seashore, thus carrying on its commendable tradition of donating lands for national parks and seashores."

In addition to the National Park Service's developing the seashore, the Army Corps of Engineers would implement its own project. The Corps proposed a $5.8 million artificial sand dune running the soundside length of the seashore, from Ocracoke Inlet to Beaufort Inlet. The dune would be built of material dredged from behind the banks, thereby forming a navigable channel one hundred feet wide from Beaufort to Ocracoke. Not only would this, as one supporter noted during a Senate hearing in 1963, provide "an invaluable boon to both sport and commercial fishermen," it would "restore and preserve a portion of the Outer Banks now threatened, [and] would strengthen the outer barrier that now protects the mainland from inundation by the sea."

Senator Bible's committee assembled newspaper articles and written communications, and heard testimony from sixteen witnesses, including U.S. Representative David N. Henderson, Senators Ervin and Jordan, and environmentalists such as Bob Simpson of the North Carolina Wildlife Federation and Louis Clapper of the National Wildlife Federation, among others. Senator Jordan noted with enthusiasm the wide support for the bill from local, state, and federal agencies. Counted among the bill's supporters was President Lyndon B. Johnson, who specifically included the Cape Lookout National Seashore as part of his program for natural resources development.

In fact, so favorable were the comments that Senator Bible noted incredulously: "I cannot overlook the opportunity of saying I cannot believe there is no one against this [bill]...If the tenor of this testimony continues, and we have no opposition whatever to it, I think it will be a first in the Halls of Congress." Woodrow Price, chairman of the North Carolina Seashore Commission, cautioned Senator Bible that he thought there might be "one or two" dissenters, but "they should speak for themselves." Price went on to state that there was "no controversy" in North Carolina over to the proposal to establish the Cape Lookout National Seashore, but he added that some "landowners whose acreage is involved are reluctant to trade off their lands and have so stated."

Then, J.M. Davis, a businessman from Morehead City, addressed the panel. He was there as an ordinary citizen and wanted the record to show that he had no objection to the creation of the national seashore park. But he wanted to point out what he called a "weakness" in the bill.

Davis owned a tract of land on Core Banks which, he was in the nation's capitol to assert, deserved the same exemption as that given to the Core Sound Gun Club. His family had owned the property for generations and, with a dozen "close friends and business associates," he too had used his one-mile stretch of dune and marshland as a hunting club. "A hunting club?" asked Senator Bible. "Yes, sir," Davis responded. "So its use is the same as the Core Banks Gun Club, actually?" the senator asked and then stated: "So we have made an exclusion of one gun club and we have not made an exclusion of yours." Davis responded that he wished to be treated "in the same manner" as the Core Banks Gun Club, and he believed that justice would prevail in "these times when there is so much discussion of...basic rights, constitutional privileges, and fair treatment."

Senator Paul J. Fannin of Arizona then struck the morning's first sour note when he said: "I am just wondering, Mr. Chairman, how many others might be in the same position you are in, Mr. Davis, that would preclude this program being carried through as originally stated." Fannin asked for assurance that the federal government would not eventually be called upon to purchase land on Core Banks that North Carolina failed to acquire. He received a vague response from Parks Icenhour, representing the State's Property Office. When asked to address the issue, Icenhour could only say: "I think funds are available to purchase the rest of the land that the State does not own to put in the fifty-eight mile tract." The matter was then dropped while testimony was heard from representatives of environmental associations. However, when A. Clark Stratton, associate director of the National Park Service, completed his statement, Senator Bible immediately asked him to "tell us about this exclusion, particularly about the Core Banks Club—why you exclude them and do not exclude Mr. Davis?"

Stratton, whose long history with the park service included helping to write the legislation for the Cape Hatteras National Seashore, then proceeded to talk at length about everything *but* the gun club exclusion. Following a second request from Senator Bible that he comment "as to why you exclude the Core Banks Gun Club and you do not exclude Mr. Davis," Stratton avoided the issue altogether and called upon his associate, Thomas Morse, who "has been quite close to this" to answer the question.

By this time apparently perturbed by Stratton's evasiveness, Bible stated that he was "impressed" by Davis's statement and added: "Let me say that I cannot understand why you treat one group one way and another group another way." Morse noted that the issue first came up in discussions in Washington in April 1963. Later, state officials and the park service held "some public hearings," including one in the Carteret County Courthouse in which the proposed development of the seashore was explained and the exclusion of the gun club was publicly mentioned "for the purpose of giving this publicity and letting anyone else who desired such treatment come forward." Morse then added: "Nobody came forward."

A self-described "old duck hunter," Senator Bible was clearly not satisfied with Morse's explanation. In fact, he seemed hostile toward him and Stratton, saying: "We find that the park service sometimes is a little ruthless in its dealing with people who have property..." He added: "Maybe I do not understand all the facts, but I do not see how you can treat the Core Banks Gun Club one way and the Davis operation, which is a gun club, another way." Acknowledging that he did not want to be "haunted" by inconsistent treatment of what appeared to be comparable entities, Bible instructed the park service to look into this "detail." He admonished Stratton and Morse saying: "I do not think this is the way to create a park."

Although he described the gun club exclusion as "one little difference" that needed to be worked out, Bible asserted that favorable opinion of the bill was "so close to unanimity that I am almost willing to say it is unanimous." In fact, though, the gun club exclusion and the exclusion of additional property adjacent to Cape Lookout Lighthouse would come close to dooming the park. At the very least, one consequence of these exclusions was that the U.S. taxpayers would pay far more dearly for their "seashore playground" than anyone, particularly the National Park Service, could have predicted. And the obvious preference shown to privileged outsiders would poison for years the relationship between the federal government and long-time residents of Carteret County.

On July 27, 1965, the Bill was approved by the Senate "without debate or dissent."[5] Predictions of House of Representatives approval by Labor Day were overly optimistic, but the measure—H.R. 1784, introduced Jan 6, 1966—came before the committee on Interior and Insular Affairs, which conducted a hearing on February 1. As was the case in the Senate, no objections were heard. Witnesses favoring the bill included W. H. "Piggie" Potter, mayor of Beaufort and chairman of the Carteret County National Seashore Park Committee, who read a statement by Carteret County attorney, Herbert O. Phillips III, saying that the Carteret County Board of Commissioners "has received no objection to the establishment of the national park." With a favorable report from the committee, the Bill won easy House approval.

On March 10, 1966, amid much fanfare and publicity, President Lyndon Johnson signed Public Law 89-366, the enabling legislation for Cape Lookout National Seashore. In the East Room of the White House, more than seventy North Carolinians and at least that many conservationists attended the ceremony and heard the president say that he wanted to be "judged as we judge the great conservationists of yesterday as benefactors of our people and as builders of a more beautiful America." *The News and Observer* reported that this was the first time in 1966 that the president put his name to a bill which he specifically requested as part of his Great Society program. "And he was apparently glad to be able to talk about something besides Viet Nam."[6]

Under the bill, the park service was authorized to establish Cape Lookout National Seashore on 30,000 acres stretching from Ocracoke Inlet in the north to Beaufort Inlet in the south. The plan was that the State of North Carolina would acquire all of Portsmouth Island and Core Banks, including Cape Lookout, and that these lands would then be turned over the federal government. By 1966, eighty percent of the acreage on Portsmouth Island and Core Banks had been purchased. Under the agreement, North Carolina would continue to acquire acreage on Core Banks and, in turn, would donate the whole package to the federal government for development. The Department of the Interior was then obligated to conduct its own buying program for Shackleford Banks. When all the land was purchased, the National Park Service could then begin to develop the seashore.

All in all, it looked as if the federal government was getting a pretty good deal. With the major cost of land acquisition being absorbed by the State of North Carolina, President Johnson would be able to add another link to the Great Society's "necklace" of National Seashore Parks extending from New England to Texas. According to National Park Service estimates, by the fifth year of operation, more than a million annual visitors living within 250 "airline miles" of the North Carolina coast would be romping through their new seashore park at Cape Lookout.

But the skepticism that arose during the 1965 Senate hearing would prove to be well-founded. The National Park Service discovered that, unlike the arrangement at Cape Hatteras, it could not administer the Cape Lookout seashore as "a single administrative unit" as excluded lands cut across strategic sections of Core Banks. And because these lands were legally excluded, it was far more difficult for the State of North Carolina to acquire them. Thus, by 1971 North Carolina still had not fulfilled its end of the bargain. Negotiations that once had seemed so positive hit snags when property owners refused to sell. The Core Banks Gun Club—whose members included a number of Greensboro attorneys—initiated complex legal proceedings designed to encumber the process even further.

The 1966 legislation was flawed not only by the exclusion of the tract belonging to the gun club, but also by the potentially more damaging exclusion of a smaller 230-acre tract owned by Charles M. Reeves, a Sanford businessman. With his property in the shadow of Cape Lookout lighthouse, Reeves planned for a residential development consisting of 796 individual lots. Legal wrangling over both of these tracts would prevent the park from being established for years and at times even threatened its existence. Seven years after President Johnson signed the authorizing legislation for the seashore park, litigation was still dragging on and led an observer to comment gloomily: "In reality, the National Seashore is only an idea, subject to be washed away like sands in a winter storm."[7] Moreover, local residents who had already been required to sell their property for the purpose of establishing the seashore deeply resented what appeared to be the special consideration afforded to outsiders. For his part, Reeves stated he had no objection to transferring his property to the government "if they are willing to pay the price for it."

Delays continued and, of course, property values steadily increased, to the delight of the litigants and the growing dismay of those who in good faith had relinquished their land for the public good and, in some instances, for less than $20 an acre. In April 1974, the State of North Carolina finally came to an agreement with Reeves, paying him $1,500,000 for his property and giving him a twenty-five-year lease on a small portion of it. Later the same year, negotiations with the Core Banks Gun Club also ended, with the club receiving $3,000,000 for real estate its appraisers had valued at $3,600,000. For their efforts, club members received about $3,000 an acre for their land, plus a lease allowing them use of part of the property for twenty-five years. Both Reeves and the gun club may have held out longer had it not been for the introduction of federal legislation that would amend the 1966 bill to include their land in the seashore. Even as their twenty-five-year lease was coming to an end, members of the Core Banks Gun Club were still trying to hang on to their institution. In November 1999, park superintendent Karren Brown indicated that the club tried "various and sundry" activities to extend the lease. These activities included inquiries from Congress and an attempt to create a non-profit corporation to operate the site as a retreat for other non-profits to visit and learn about waterfowl history. All of these efforts were unsuccessful and when the lease expired on November 23, 1999, the gun club land finally reverted to the public trust.[8]

The original 1966 Cape Lookout National Seashore legislation authorized an amount "not to exceed" $3,200,000 for park development and land acquisition, including Shackleford Banks. In 1974, the amount was raised to $7,903,000 for land acquisition alone. Although nearly twice that amount would eventually be needed before all necessary land was in the hands of the federal government, the acquisition of the gun club and Reeves tracts allowed the project to move forward. In a formal gathering of national and state officials in June at the Cape Lookout Lighthouse, North Carolina Governor James Holshauser officially transferred to the federal government approximately 28,000 acres of state-owned land on Core Banks and Portsmouth Island. If everything proceeded as expected, the Cape Lookout National Seashore could now be officially established. The federal government could begin acquiring Shackleford Banks, and could develop a management plan for the seashore.

(ABOVE) *This restored bread delivery truck has been modified to use airplane tires, which give it superior ability to operate over sand with the least amount of disruption to the road and beach surface. Mounted on the roof (behind the pick-up truck bed cap) is a black plastic water tank for hot showers.*
(photo by Carmine Prioli)

(BELOW) *For greater mobility in spotting and chasing fish along the Banks, some fishermen use all-terrain vehicles, adapted to hold tackle and other equipment.* (photo by Carmine Prioli)

Soon after the establishment of the Seashore, the National Park Service conducted two public workshops (in Raleigh and Morehead City) from which there evolved in 1978 five alternative plans for the park's management and use. Park service officials interpreted public response to the plans to mean that the seashore should be managed predominantly as a wilderness area. Thus, on August 1, 1980, park superintendent Preston "Mack" Riddel released a plan that proposed wilderness designation for Core Banks north of Shingle Point, Portsmouth Island (except for Portsmouth Village), and Shackleford Banks. This meant that development of the area would be virtually prohibited. It also meant that all structures and private motor vehicles—like the ones that surf fishermen had been ferrying over to Core Banks since the 1940s—would be banned. The only motorized transport allowable would be a public system operating between Cape Lookout Point to Shingle Point, a distance of fourteen miles.

Opposition to the plan was immediate and vocal. Surf fishermen, especially, saw the prohibition against private vehicles as the virtual elimination of their sport, because they needed the mobility provided by their beach buggies to track the fish. Waiting for a public transport vehicle to move fishermen to hot spots that could appear and then disappear within minutes anywhere along a fifty-mile strand was scorned as a ridiculous and unrealistic alternative. Neither could fishermen be expected to carry coolers, fishing tackle, and other gear to and from remote locations. Surf fishermen rallied the support of similar groups from across the United States. At four public hearings in September 1980, they were the dominant presence, offering the park service several hundred oral and written statements. Additionally, they submitted a petition requesting that Cape Lookout National Seashore "provide specifically for the use of private vehicles in a controlled fashion on Core Banks and Portsmouth Island, and in this way retain for surf fishermen an experience which cannot be duplicated on any shoreline in the nation." The petition also suggested that Shackleford Banks be designated as wilderness. It contained 14,000 signatures.

Local and statewide agencies, including the North Carolina Marine Fisheries Commission, opposed the wilderness designation for Core Banks and favored "controlled use of private vehicles." Elected officials, including Governor James B. Hunt and Senator Jesse Helms, also rallied to the side of surf fishermen. U.S. Representative Walter B. Jones stated: "To deprive these good citizens [fishermen and hunters] the right to utilize that equipment essential to the pursuit of their favorite sport will result in a very unfair situation and one which I will vigorously oppose at all levels of review."[9]

No one at this point opposed wilderness designation for Shackleford Banks. In fact, nearly everyone who publicly voiced opposition to the banning of motor vehicles on Core Banks specifically supported the ban (and the wilderness designation) for Shackleford. Typical of such state-

Beach buggies are restored older vehicles that have been modified for living and fishing along the Banks. Many are shared by several individuals and show their owners' remarkable skill in creating innovative and efficient campers that are entirely self-contained and environmentally friendly.
(photos by Carmine Prioli)

ments was that of Senator Helms who wrote to Russell E. Dickenson, director of the National Park Service: "It has been suggested that Shackleford Banks be designated as wilderness since its use by the public has been minimal. This seems reasonable and a proposal which I would have no difficulty supporting provided Core Banks and Portsmouth Island are allowed to remain in the natural state and open to the controlled use of private vehicles."[10] The official position of the State of North Carolina was that "only Shackleford should be recommended to Congress for wilderness designation."[11]

As a result of the pressure, park officials rejected the arguments of such conservation groups as the American Wilderness Alliance and the Audubon Naturalist Society. They revised their plan and offered a "compromise" that would allow restricted vehicular access along a specified beach corridor of Core Banks, while Shackleford Banks would become entirely a wilderness area. Since surf fishing with motorized vehicles was never widely practiced on Shackleford, the surf fishermen—non-Carteret County residents for the most part—had scored an important and lasting victory. Years later, Superintendent Riddel described the motor vehicle controversy on Core Banks as the "big issue" in developing Cape Lookout.[12]

While the park service was working on its management plan, it was also moving ahead with efforts to acquire Shackleford Banks and thereby own all of the land necessary for the seashore. On January 30, 1978, the federal government filed condemnation proceedings in U.S. District Court in New Bern to obtain clear title to the 2,369 acres of Shackleford and another 2,000 or so acres of adjacent marshland. The process was complicated by the fact that ownership of significant portions of the island was uncertain. A few months later, U.S. Attorney George Anderson told citizens gathered in the Harkers Island Elementary School that his office in Raleigh had served papers on 154 persons—most of them residents of Carteret County—with potential ownership interests. He pointed out, however, that not all of the defendants were likely to have legitimate claims to ownership. In fact, only a few of the approximately three-score cottages on the Banks actually stood on land owned by their builders. Most of the owners of those cottages therefore faced the ominous prospect of eviction from land that had been an important part of their lives for many years.

According to the criteria established in the 1966 legislation, twenty-five-year leases could be given only to legal owners of property within the seashore if (1) the property was owned on January 1, 1966, and (2) it was developed for non-commercial purposes on July 1, 1963. There was no allowance for "third party" claims, that is, claims of individuals whose right to use the property was based upon the stated or implied permission of the legal owners. In some cases, where it was not clear that anyone owned a particular piece of property, claims were made

The Wild Horses of Shackleford Banks

Carmine Prioli

"There has been domestic livestock grazing on Shackleford Banks since the 18th century. Even when the State of North Carolina outlawed grazing of livestock on the Outer Banks (1958) they exempted Shackleford Banks. In accordance with the Park's General Management Plan, cows, sheep and goats will be removed, but because of their potentially historic origin, a 'representative' herd of horses will remain on Shackleford."

—from "Statement for Management: Cape Lookout National Seashore" (revised, July 1987)

simply on the basis that the land had been developed or built upon and the builder therefore had some legal right to it.

Ownership of portions of Shackleford property was clouded over the years by a number of factors. Some deeds were improperly recorded or never recorded at all. Others were inexact or overlapping in their descriptions. Some ancient deeds were lost altogether and, of course, nature's processes had a predictable effect on property boundaries. Geographical alterations caused by wave action transformed what was oceanfront property into vast expanses of sea water. In the same process, new soundside property was created, where once only salt water and marshland existed.*

Legal proceedings dragged on until 1985, when Shackleford was finally added to the seashore park, culminating a process that took nearly two decades since the time President Johnson signed the enabling legislation. Ultimately, the courts determined that only about a dozen individuals possessed legal rights to Shackleford real estate. Because of the time that passed, property values rose far beyond what the government had originally anticipated. In 1966, the estimated cost for purchasing Shackleford Banks was approximately $161,000. Although that was probably low even for 1966, no one could have foreseen that the eventual cost to the taxpayers would exceed $8,000,000.

Only two structures on the island qualified for twenty-five-year leases. The remaining buildings, ranging from makeshift shelters to multi-bedroom cottages, would have to be removed, for, according to park service guidelines, designating Shackleford as wilderness required that the imprint of all human activity be "substantially absent." This mandated not only the eradication of structures deemed inconsistent with the wilderness quality, but also the removal of domesticated animals—sheep, goats, and cattle—defined as "exotic," that is, not indigenous to the area. Bowing to what they rightly perceived as strong local sentiment, park officials determined that an exception would be made for the hundred or so feral horses that roamed the Banks in

*For a discussion of the dynamic nature of North Carolina's coastal boundaries, see Stanley R. Riggs's essay, "Life at the Edge of North Carolina's Coastal System: The Geologic Controls," in this volume, pp. 63–95.

*B*y the summer of 1994, the herd of feral horses that the National Park Service had allowed to roam Shackleford since 1985 had grown from one hundred to 224. Park officials feared that the size of the herd had now reached starvation levels. They also believed that by overgrazing on salt marsh cordgrass, sea oats, and other vegetation necessary for preventing erosion, the herd was exerting an adverse environmental impact on the island. These were the chief factors that led to the creation of a management plan specifically for the horses. The object was to reduce the herd drastically with a one-time round-up and removal: all horses would be checked for equine infectious anemia (EIA), and those stricken with this incurable disease would be put down as required by state law. A few remaining horses would be removed for possible adoption on the mainland, and a small number (fifty-sixty) would remain on the island. Population would be controlled by sterilization of some of the males and by annually shooting some of the mares with birth control darts.

Many locals were convinced that the National Park Service's real aim was to eventually remove all of the horses. They believe that these animals are descendants of shipwrecked Spanish mustangs that swam onto the Shackleford beaches as early as 1565. Removing them would erase one of the New World's oldest living legacies as well as one of Cape Lookout's main tourist attractions.

In early 1996, several hundred residents signed a petition stating, "We cannot stand idly

Pony roundup, July 4, 1979. Note Banker cottages in the background. (photo by Ken Taylor)

by and allow this important segment of our natural and cultural history to be destroyed." Some Down Easters wanted to care for the horses themselves by reviving the tradition of July 4th community round-ups where the ponies were penned temporarily, new colts and fillies were branded, and those in need were given medical attention. Others were vocal in their outright opposition to the park service's plan. In March 1996, gathering on Beaufort's courthouse lawn, they staged a rally "to educate and encourage those who love the idea of the Shackleford Banks horses, which have run wild for 400 years, to continue to have that freedom."

Eventually bowing a bit to the pressure, park service officials agreed to maintain a larger herd of about one hundred horses. But they proceeded with their original design. Using hired wranglers and border collies, an airplane, all-terrain vehicles and horses, they rounded up 184 Shackleford ponies in a single day in November. Seventy-six tested positive for EIV, were removed and euthanized with drugs. These horses were unceremoniously buried in a landfill on the mainland. While some horsebreeders and veterinarians saw the killing of the horses as a sad necessity, the manner in which it was carried out further strengthened the movement to wrest control of the remaining horses from the National Park Service. Out of the controversy came an organization—the Foundation for Shackleford Horses—and H.R. 765, a congressional act "To ensure maintenance of a herd of wild horses in Cape Lookout National Seashore."

Sponsored by Representative Walter B. Jones, Jr., representing North Carolina's 3rd Congressional district, H.R. 765 proposed that a herd of not fewer than one hundred to 110 horses be exempted from the National Park Service's "exotic" animal policy. This policy dictates the removal of non-native animal species from park service land designated as a wilderness area. Further, Rep. Jones' act required the National Park Service to "enter into an agreement with the Foundation for Shackleford Horses…to provide for management of free roaming horses in the seashore."

Public-private partnerships are not entirely uncommon in some national parks, but such an arrangement dealing with the preservation of a non-native species was one the National Park Service opposed as a "disturbing precedent." This opposition had little effect in the U.S. House of Representatives. When H.R. 765 was brought before the assembly on July 22, 1997, it passed, 416 to six. When it became apparent that President Clinton would sign the bill (at the urging of Erskine Bowles, the President's White House chief of staff at the time) the National Park Service announced that it would not oppose H.R. 765. Subsequently, with the support of Senator Jesse Helms, the bill won easy approval in the Senate and was signed by President Clinton on July 9, 1998.

Thus, H.R. 765 amended the Congressional act that established Cape Lookout National Seashore in 1966 by ensuring the wild horses a permanent presence on the Shackleford Banks seascape. But the Jones bill did more—it transformed the horses into living emblems of a bedrock American principle. As the *Carteret County News-Times* asserted, the pony controversy showed that "a determined people with a righteous cause can fight city hall, or in this case Uncle Sam, and win." And this, the editorial concluded, "is what democracy is all about."

several herds. Popular tradition maintains that these animals were actually descendants of horses brought to the New World several hundred years earlier by Spanish explorers.

Most upsetting to some Harkers Island residents, however, was the mandated removal of their cottages, some of which had been erected at considerable expense in recent years. On July 7, 1985, the National Park Service published the following announcement in local newspapers:

> Notice is hereby given that all structures, livestock, other animals and other personal property on Shackleford Banks not authorized or permitted by the United States must be removed by midnight, December 31, 1985. Persons leaving unauthorized or unpermitted structures, animals or other personal property on the Island past the above deadline relinquish any claim to the same.

Another notice appeared a few days before the December 31 deadline.

Although the government was within its rights to issue such notices, local residents considered the approach high-handed and insensitive to the preservation of their lifestyle and heritage. Park officials still had vivid memories of the complications that had ensued several years earlier in 1975, when squatters on Core Banks came close to dooming the national seashore. Having erected ramshackle huts by the hundreds on land the state of North Carolina was planning to turn over to the federal government, these individuals hoped to secure twenty-five-year leases to property they claimed to have "developed." In reality, most of the Core Banks squatters' huts were crude shelters built of scrap materials and scattered along the Banks in clusters of units, surrounded by years of accumulated trash: litter, old appliances, and more than 2,500 abandoned and rusting motor vehicles lay in the sand defacing the length and breadth of the island.[13]

Neither the government nor the state wanted to deal with the squatters. "As I look at it," declared Superintendent Riddel at the time, "the state has acquired the land beneath the structures and now has the responsibility to do something with the improvements thereon." Then he added: "I am not going to be a part of this."[14] Clearly, the responsibility was North Carolina's and after months of equivocation, the state proceeded with the evictions. The whole matter was a public relations nightmare that, especially during an election year, was not welcomed by state office holders.

So when national park officials were faced with dealing with those they considered Shackleford Banks squatters, their approach was straightforward and unbending: only those structures that fulfilled the letter of the requirements set out in the enabling

Rusted remains of one of the many vehicles abandoned on Core Banks. Although more than 2,500 of these hulks were removed, the likelihood of environmental damage caused by heavy equipment required that many remain to be alternately buried and uncovered by the shifting sands.
(photo by Carmine Prioli)

legislation would remain. There were, however, crucial differences between the land grab that had earlier been attempted on Core Banks and the camps that, in some cases, had existed for years on Shackleford. The Shackleford community was largely a collection of local families, many of them descendants of Ca'e Bankers. They practiced a tradition of gentle land use that contrasted with the exploitation or outright despoliation of the environment practiced by many of the weekend surf fishermen on Core Banks. Piedmont residents for the most part, the surf fishermen were basically out-of-towners who ferried their vehicles to the Banks two or three times annually. The Shackleford visitors came year-round to sail, swim, fish, clam, tend gardens and livestock, and maintain for themselves and their children a remnant of the lifestyle of their ancestors.

Although many of the Bankers had no deeds to the land, they claimed "residence" based on emotional ties to the island that for generations had been considered communal property. Their Shackleford camps were not just weekend retreats. They were extensions of their primary homes and, most important, their camps connected them spiritually with a past that was increasingly threatened by the tourism and commercialism that were rapidly overrunning their mainland environments.

As the time neared when Bankers would have to abandon their Shackleford camps, a series of mysterious fires occurred that symbolized local anger. In December 1985, night skies were brightened by the glow of flaming cottages on Shackleford. To older eyes, the view from Harkers Island and the mainland was reminiscent of the glow on the horizon of burning ships torpedoed by German U-boats in World War II.

Some of the cottages were torched by their owners. Others, including the two belonging to individuals—Mildred Holland and Edna Bjerke of Beaufort—who were given twenty-five-year leases, were burned illegally. Most serious of all was the destruction, in the early morning hours of December 30, 1985, of the Cape Lookout National Seashore visitors' center on the eastern end of Harkers Island. Superintendent Riddel acknowledged hearing talk that "somebody was going to do something,"[15] but no one was prepared for the burning of the center. In addition to the $100,000 structure, data collected in wildlife research—including six years of loggerhead turtle studies—was destroyed.

Subsequent investigations by local authorities determined that the fire had been intentionally set. Although the F.B.I. was brought into the case and two rewards of several thousand dollars each were offered, no one was ever charged with the burning. Eventually, all of the remaining structures on Shackleford were removed, either

Remains of burned-out cottage on Shackleford Banks. Note overturned sink in foreground. Houseboats moored in background show how some Bankers have continued their camp tradition. (photo by Carmine Prioli)

by their owners or the park service. The visitors' center was rebuilt and, in 1993, the park service opened its new regional office on Harkers Island. But the fires that burned in December 1985 left emotional wounds on both sides that have been slow to heal. The islanders felt that park officials were uncommunicative outsiders more concerned with preserving sea turtles and other forms of wildlife than with their heritage. National park officials, on the other hand, saw islanders as clannish and resentful of their efforts to preserve the islands from commercial development, thereby saving the geographical essence of Banker heritage.

Hard feelings persist, but in recent years, islanders have come to accept and see some of the benefits of the national seashore. A few have made efforts to work with park officials to establish, on U.S. property, a structure that could symbolize a new spirit of cooperation between local citizens and the federal government. On October 16, 1993, park officials and members of the Core Sound Decoy Carvers Guild endorsed a "Memorandum of Understanding" that included a seventy-five-year leasing agreement for sixteen acres of land at Shell Point, on the eastern tip of Harkers Island. The property is now the site of the Core Sound Waterfowl Museum.

The ceremonial groundbreaking for the museum occurred on January 25, 1997, and construction began in 1999. Previews of what's to come have been offered annually in the educational exhibits, crafts displays, and local history presentations that the museum has presented in its unfinished building during the 1999, 2000, and 2001 Harkers Island decoy and waterfowl festivals. According to the museum's board of directors, the structure is a "working-man's museum," bringing together historical, artistic, environmental, and educational programs. The Core Sound Waterfowl Museum also signifies for the region an invigorating spirit of cooperation between local citizens and the National Park Service. It represents a new and more positive chapter in the often-stormy history of Cape Lookout National Seashore.

Core Sound Waterfowl Museum at Shell Point on Harkers Island. (courtesy of Core Sound Waterfowl Museum)

ENDNOTES

1. Dyan Zaslowsky and The Wilderness Society. *These American Lands: Parks, Wilderness, and the Public Lands* (NY: Henry Holt & Co., 1986), pp. 31–32.

2. "Outer Banks Sought for National Seashore." *The Washington Post*, February 19, 1965.

3. Terry Sanford to Stewart Udall, March 3, 1964, microfilm reel #1, "Park Management History," Cape Lookout National Seashore (CALO) Archives, Harkers Island, NC.

4. This and all subsequent statements made during the June 3, 1965 Senate hearing are quoted from *Hearing before the Subcommittee on Parks and Recreation of the Committee on Interior and Insular Affairs on S. 251, Eighty-Ninth Congress* (U.S. Government Printing Office, Washington: 1965), p. 1.

5. "Senate Approval Boost to Carteret." *The News and Observer* (Raleigh), July 29, 1965.

6. "Seashore Bill Is Signed." *The News and Observer* (Raleigh), March 11, 1966.

7. "Seashore Plan Foundering." *Twin City Sentinel* (Winston-Salem), July 29, 1973.

8. "Down East Institution Ends With End of Lease for Rod and Gun Club." *Carteret County News-Times*, December 1, 1999.

9. Written statement contained in September 23, 1980, microfilm reel #1, "Park Management History," CALO Archives, Harkers Island, NC.

10. Jesse Helms to Russell E. Dickenson, October 14, 1980, microfilm reel #1, "Park Management," CALO Archives, Harkers Island, NC.

11. Anne Taylor to Chrys Baggett, October 10, 1980, microfilm reel #1, CALO Archives, Harkers Island, NC.

12. Joel Bourne. "A Question of Management." *Maritime Magazine*, August 14, 1986.

13. After several years and a number of failed attempts, many of the abandoned vehicles were removed. In the final stage of the operation, U.S. Marines cooperated with state and federal officials to airlift tons of rusting cars and trucks off of Core Banks. Many vehicles that were half-buried in the sand were left behind, because removing them would cause more damage to the surrounding environment than leaving them in place.

14. "Core Banks Cleanup Becomes a 'Hot Potato' For State, U.S." *Greensboro Daily News*, June 29, 1975.

15. "FBI Investigates Fires on Outer Banks." *Daily News* (Washington, NC), December 31, 1985.

Acknowledgment: The author thanks David Cecelski, Preston "Mack" Riddel, former superintendent of Cape Lookout National Seashore, and park rangers Laurie Heupel and Karen Duggan for their help with this article.

Contributors

Candy Beal is an Assistant Professor of Curriculum and Instruction at North Carolina State University. She has directed the Southern Coastal Heritage Program's "Life at the Edge of the Sea" summer workshop for educators since its inception in 1993. She is a member of NCSU's Academy of Outstanding Teachers. Her publications include (with John Arnold) *Service With A Smile: Service Learning Projects in North Carolina Middle Schools* (1995) and *Raleigh: The First 200 Years and 200 Facts for 200 Years* (1992).

James W. Clark, Jr. is a Professor of English at North Carolina State University and director of NCSU's Humanities Extension/Publications Program. He is a recipient of NCSU's Alexander Quarles Holladay Medal of Excellence. His publications include *The Lost Boy: A Novella by Thomas Wolfe* (1992), *Talking About Raleigh: A Bicentennial Oral History* (1993), and *Clover All Over: North Carolina 4-H in Action* (1984).

I. Randolph Daniel, Jr. is an Assistant Professor of Anthropology at East Carolina University. He is the recipient of the 1999 C.B. Moore Award for Excellence in Archaeology by a Young Scholar in Southeastern Studies presented by the Lower Mississippi Survey, a collaborative Tulane University-Harvard University research group. His recent publications include "Stone Raw Material and Early Archaic Settlement in the Southeastern United States" (2001), "Paleoindian Points in North Carolina" (2000), and *Hardaway Revisited: Early Archaic Settlement in the Southeast* (1998).

David Griffith is Senior Scientist and Associate Professor of Anthropology at East Carolina University. His publications include *The Estuary's Gift: An Atlantic Coast Cultural Biography* (1999), (with Donald Stull and Michael Broadway) *Any Way You Cut It: Meat Processing and Small-Town America* (1995), (with Ed Kissam) *Working Poor: Farm Workers in the United States* (1995), and *Jones's Minimal: Low-Wage Labor in the United States* (1993).

Carmine Prioli is a Professor of English at North Carolina State University. He has received NCSU awards for outstanding teaching and extension service. His publications include *"Hope for a good season": The Ca'e Bankers of Harkers Island* (1998) and *Lines of Fire: The Poetry of General George S. Patton, Jr.* (1992).

Stanley R. Riggs is Emeritus Professor of Geology and Distinguished Professor of the College of Arts and Sciences at East Carolina University. His publications include "Sediment Evolution and Habitat Function of Organic-Rich Muds within the Albemarle Estuarine System" (1996), (with S.W. Snyder, A.C. Hine, and D.L. Mearns) "Hardbottom Morphology and Relationship to the Geologic Framework of Onslow Bay, North Carolina Continental Shelf" (1996), (with W.J. Cleary and S.W. Snyder) "Influence of Inherited Geologic Framework upon Barrier Beach Morphology and Shoreface Dynamics" (1995), and (with W.C. Burnett, eds.) *Neogene to Modern Phosphorites* (1990).

Lundie Spence is Marine Education Specialist in the UNC Sea Grant College Program at North Carolina State University. She is the recipient of the NOAA Environmental Hero Award for 2000. Her publications include (with D. Thorpe) *What Supervisors Need to Know about Field Trips and Liability* (1993), "Accessing Marine Education Curriculum Materials" (1990), (with V. Coxe) "Coastal Capers: A Marine Education Primer" (1985), and (with Jack Wheatley and G. Jones) "Studying Characteristics of Successful Student/Teacher Interaction in Marine Science Projects" (1985).

Walt Wolfram is Professor of English and William C. Friday Professor of Socio-Linguistics at North Carolina State University. His publications include (with Erik Thomas) *The Development of African American English* (2002), (with Kirk Hazen and Natalie Schilling-Estes) *Dialect Maintenance and Change on the Outer Banks* (1999), and (with Natalie Schilling-Estes) *Hoi Toide on the Outer Banks: The Story of the Ocracoke Brogue* (1997).